CHINA

WORLD HERITAGE SITES

CHINA

WORLD HERITAGE SITES

CAO NANYAN

MINISTRY OF CONSTRUCTION OF THE P.R.C., CHINA NATIONAL
COMMISSION FOR UNESCO AND STATE BUREAU OF CULTURAL RELICS
OF THE P.R.C.

中国的世界遗产 / 曹南燕 主编

© 2003 China Architecture & Building Press,
Baiwanzhuang, 100037 Beijing, China

This 2008 edition published by

COMPENDIUM

© 2008 by Compendium Publishing Ltd.
43 Frith Street, Soho, London, W1D 4SA, UK

Editor: Claire Welch
Design: Peran Publishing Services
Chief Editor: Cao Nanyan
Deputy Chief Editors: Ma Yansheng, Jing Feng,
    Guo Zhan
Text: Yang Gusheng, Cao Nanyan, Wu Yujiang
English Translations: Mo Runxian, He Fei, Hu
    Zhongping, Zhang Long, Pan Jingyi
English Editors: Liang Liangxing, Kai Lin
Major Photographers: Wan Guoqing, Wang Jie,
    Wang Jinghui, Wei Ran, Liu Yuqing, Wang
    Mingyi, Li Dongxi, Yang Gusheng, Wu
    Tianhao, Zhang Zhengguang, Zhang Zhaoji,
    Chen Xiaoli, Chen Baosen, Chen Suwei, Chen
    Yaodong, Lin Meng, Luo Yang, Luo Zhewen,
    Zhao Huiting, Qian Zhenyue, Ni Murong, Cao
    Yang, Huang Bin, Cui Guihai, Xiong
    Yuansheng, Xiong Qirui.

ISBN: 978-1-905573-39-4

Printed and bound in China

This book was prepared by Compendium
Publishing Limited using material from China
Architecture and Building Press originally
published as World Heritage Sites of China.

PAGE 1: The Great Wall at Jiumenkou Pass. The
name Jiumenkou literally means "Entrance to
Nine Gates."

PAGES 2–3: The moat, palace city wall, and corner
tower of the Imperial Palace of the Ming and
Qing dynasties in Beijing.

RIGHT: Wenchangge Tower, one of the four
similar buildings in the Summer Palace shaped like
city gates.

PAGE 6: The Seventeen-Arch Bridge—at 492ft in
length it is the largest and longest stone bridge in
the Summer Palace.

CONTENTS

INTRODUCTION

INTRODUCTION

China's culture is deeply rooted in the main factors that determine World Heritage Site inclusion. All over the country can be found masterpieces of cultural history and majestic natural scenic areas—treasures that have been recognized as being of not just national but world importance such as the Great Wall, the Terra-cotta Army, and the Peking Man Site at Zhoukoudian.

The combined notions of culture and nature are fundamental to Chinese civilization. Natural beauties inspired political and religious leaders, philosophers, writers, poets, artists, and people from all walks of life. This is embodied in the cultural creativity of the sites. Ancestor worship and animist religions, practiced by the diverse peoples of the vast territory that make up China today, contribute to make the veneration of nature and culture the very essence of Chinese civilization.

With the ratification of the Convention concerning the Protection of World Cultural and Natural Heritage in 1985, the Chinese Government attached enormous importance to the conservation of these properties. The Chinese sites included on the prestigious World Heritage

List are outstanding examples of human genius and master works of humanity.

This publication marks the thirty-second anniversary of the adoption of the World Heritage Convention by UNESCO's General Conference. A hundred and seventy-five countries ratified this Convention, which makes it the most universal international legal body for heritage conservation.

The Convention is uniquely founded on the premise that certain natural and cultural sites are of "outstanding universal value" and form part of the common heritage of humankind. The conservation of this common heritage is of concern not just for individual nations, but for all humanity. Another unique feature of the convention is that it seeks to protect both cultural and natural heritage. In view of the many links between culture and nature, this holistic approach has set new standards for heritage protection.

A system of international co-operation and assistance has been established with support from the World Heritage Fund. At the biennial General Assembly of States Parties to the Convention, a twenty-one-member inter-governmental World Heritage Committee is elected.

Under the World Heritage Convention, implementation work is carried out by the UNESCO World Heritage Center as Secretariat. The International

BELOW LEFT: Houzaimen Gate at Mount Taishan's Daimiao Temple. Emperors used to hold ceremonies at this temple paying their respect to Taishan before their ascent to the top of the mountain.

BELOW: Snow on the limestone formations enhance the colorful pools at Huanglong. The area was included in the UNESCO World Heritage List in 1992.

Council of Monuments and Sites (ICOMOS), the International Union for Conservation of Nature and Natural Resources (IUCN), and the International Center for the Study of the Preservation and Restoration of Cultural Property (ICCROM) act as Advisory Bodies. ICOMOS, a non-governmental organization (founded by UNESCO in 1965), assists the World Heritage Committee in the evaluation and selection of cultural sites for the World Heritage List. IUCN (set up by UNESCO in 1948), advises the Committee on the selection and conservation of natural heritage sites. In addition, ICCROM (created by UNESCO in 1965 and based in Rome), provides expert advice on the restoration of cultural properties and training. The Convention also includes in the World Heritage List the "combined works of nature and man."

In December 1992, the Committee adopted criteria for the acceptance of cultural landscapes as World Heritage sites. Both ICOMOS and IUCN review nominations for such sites.

Every year the World Heritage Committee approves emergency assistance under the World Heritage Fund to World Heritage sites. This includes funds for sites severely damaged by natural disaster or human-related deterioration, for conservation training, and to identify and nominate properties for inclusion on the prestigious UNESCO World Heritage List.

So far, 721 sites of outstanding universal value have been included on the list. Of these sites, 554 are cultural, 144 are natural, and 23 are mixed cultural and natural sites. They are located in 125 countries. Many of these sites are now threatened and considerable efforts are required to ensure their continued conservation.

BELOW: The mountain resort and its outlying temples in Chengde, Hebei Province, was listed as a World Heritage Site in 1994.

RIGHT: These terracotta warriors and horses, a few of the estimated 7,000 such figures, have watched over Qin Shi Huang's Mausoleum in Shaanxi Province for more than 2,000 years.

LEFT: The Hall of Prayer for Good Harvests at Beijing's Temple of Heaven, originally built in 1420.

BELOW LEFT: Rock carvings dating from the ninth to the thirteenth century at Dazu, the harmonious synthesis of Buddhism, Taoism, and Confucianism.

BELOW: The Summer Palace's Grand Theater was built in 1895 to celebrate the Empress Dowager Cixi's sixtieth birthday.

THE GREAT WALL

THE GREAT WALL

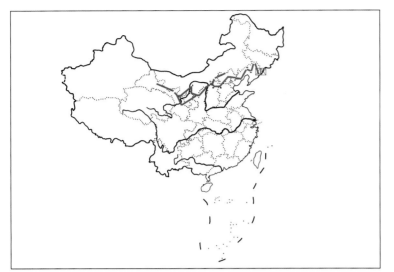

LOCATION: North China. The Great Wall of the Ming period extends from Liaoning Province in the east to Gansu Province in the west.

REGISTERED: 1987 (cultural site), expanding to the Jiumenkou section in 2002.

The Great Wall of China starts in the distant east beside the Yalu River, stretches westward through Tianjin, then travels toward Beijing, Hebei, Inner Mongolia, Shanxi, Shaanxi, Ningxia, and Gansu, before ending at the Jiayuguan Pass. It is an amalgamation of a number of different defensive walls, constructed at different times on the orders of a variety of kings and emperors all with the intention of keeping out foreign invaders.

Most of the walls we see today date back to the Ming period, although the earliest bits can be traced back to the ninth century B.C. in the Zhou period, when King Xuanwang built a series of walls and beacon towers to defend his kingdom against the northern tribes. Then, during the seventh century B.C., many princedoms—such as Qi, Wei, Zhao, Yan and Qin—built their own long defensive walls to defend their lands from aggressors.

Shortly after his conquest of the six states and unification of the whole country in 221 B.C., Qin Shi Huang—the first emperor of the Qin Dynasty—ordered

PREVIOUS PAGES: The grandeur of the Jinshanling section of the Great Wall, which takes its name from the Jinshan Mountains, is apparent in this photograph. Initial construction took place between 1368 and 1389 during the Ming Dynasty.

LEFT: The Eastern Gate Tower of Shanhaiguan Pass bears an inscription that reads "The First Pass Under Heaven" and houses a collection of ancient military uniforms and weapons.

ABOVE: The Great Wall on Jiaoshan Mountain at Shanhaiguan Pass. Jiaoshan Mountain, along with Changshou Mountain and Yansai Lake, make up the Shanhaiguan District historical site.

the construction of a great wall, to incorporate the existing long walls. In the north of the former Qin, Yan, and Zhao states the walls were enlarged, extended, and linked to form the Qin Great Wall that started from Lintao in the west and ran to Liaodong in the east. During the Han Dynasty at Emperor Wudi's orders, walls were also built and rebuilt to guard Hetao, western Gansu, and other regions and routes important for east–west trade and movement.

The amount of work put into the construction of the Great Wall is astonishing: the wall erected in the Ming period alone is estimated to contain enough brick, stone, and earth to build a road thirty-three feet wide and fourteen inches thick round the Earth more than twice.

TOP: Linlulou Tower at Shanhaiguan Pass, the first strategic pass at the eastern end of the Great Wall and defender of Beijing and Chang'an.

ABOVE: The Lesser Square Fortification, Yumenguan (Jade Gate) Pass, on the Western Han Great Wall.

RIGHT: The Great Wall at Jiumenkou Pass used to provide the only access between northern and central China.

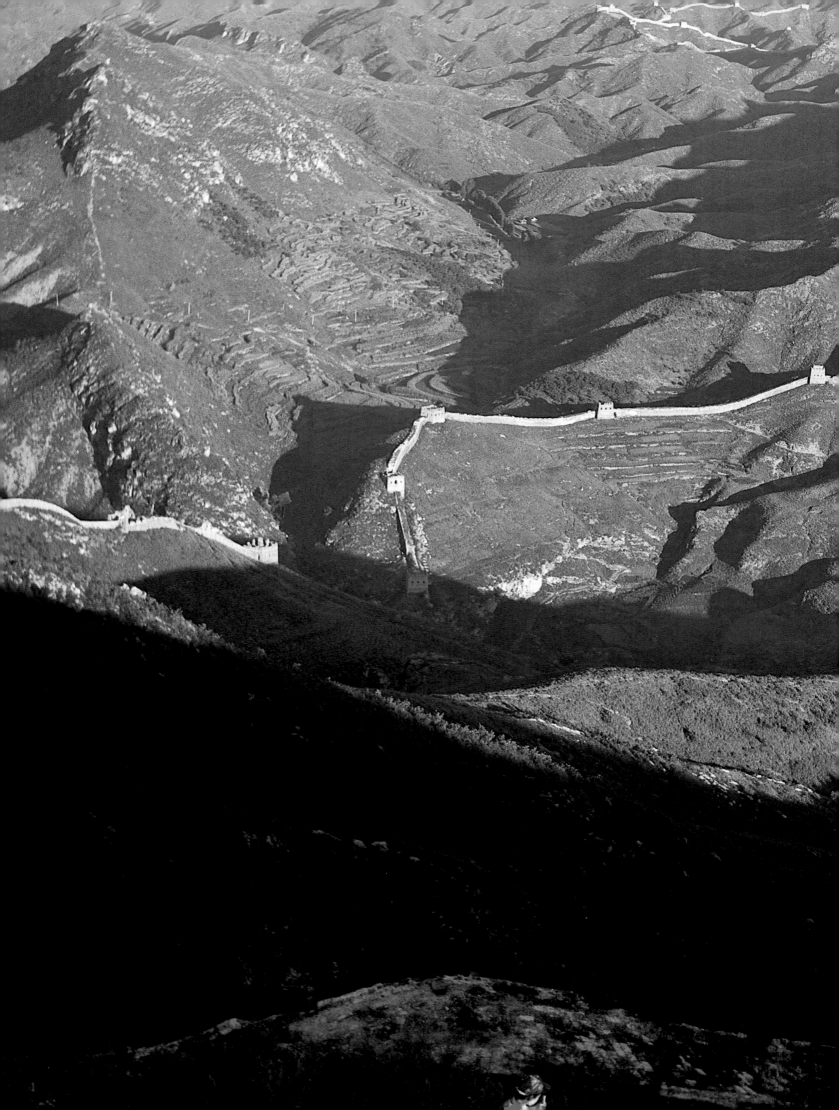

PREVIOUS PAGES: The Jinshanling section of the Great Wall as seen from Simatai. This section is second only to the Badaling Great Wall in its completeness.

RIGHT: Entrance to the Lesser Square Fortification, the Western Han Great Wall. The Western Han period lasted from 206 B.C. until 9 A.D.

OPPOSITE: Yanmenguan Pass (ABOVE) and the Gateway to Pingxingguan Pass (BELOW), built during the Northern Qi Dynasty (550–577 A.D.).

ABOVE: Corner tower and embrasured watchtower at Jiayuguan Pass, built at the western end of the Great Wall during the Ming Dynasty (1368–1644).

RIGHT: The Great Wall at Dajingmen Gate, Zhangjiakou, once marked China's northern border.

FAR RIGHT: Gate tower at Shanhaiguan Pass with a Ming Dynasty gun in the foreground.

LEFT: Ningwuguan Pass, scene of a fierce battle in 1644 when rebel peasants defeated the soldiers stationed there.

ABOVE: The first section of the Great Wall opened for tourists here on Badaling Mountain.

ABOVE: Entrance of one of the twenty-two watchtowers spaced at regular intervals on the Mutianyu section of the Great Wall.

RIGHT: Juyongguan Pass—one of the four Devarajas (god kings) on the Cloud Terrace, which dates back as early as 1345.

FAR RIGHT: Wangjinglou Tower (also known as Watching Beijing Tower) as seen from the Fairy Tower, Simatai.

IMPERIAL PALACE OF THE MING AND QING DYNASTIES

IMPERIAL PALACE OF THE MING AND QING DYNASTIES

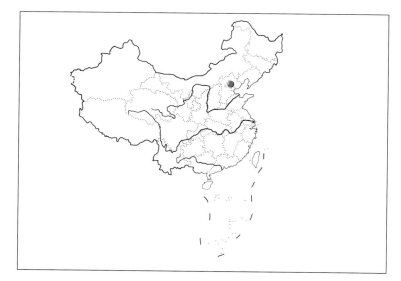

LOCATION: Center of Beijing.
REGISTERED: 1987 (cultural site).

PREVIOUS PAGES: The 170ft. wide moat, palace city wall, and corner tower of the Imperial Palace. Construction began in 1406.

The Imperial Palace of the Ming and Qing dynasties —the Forbidden City—lies at the center of Beijing. The largest collection of preserved ancient wooden structures in the world, it contains some 980 buildings, of which more than ninety date back to the Ming period. The complex is the largest and most perfectly preserved of the ancient imperial palaces remaining in the world, and is a masterpiece of ancient Chinese architecture.

The Imperial Palace was closely guarded and fortified within three city walls, those of the Forbidden City, the Imperial City, and of Beijing itself. The Imperial Palace was divided into a southern, or front section, and a northern, or back section. The front was the outer court, where the emperor exercized his authority, granted audiences to his ministers, accepted gifts, and conducted grand ceremonies. The back section was the emperor's private living quarters, where the imperial family lived in the palaces along the axis—while the concubines, princes, and other important people resided in the six western and six eastern palaces.

LEFT: The emperor's living room at the back of Yangxindian Hall where most of the emperors lived and attended to state affairs.

ABOVE: Stone carvings on the imperial steps in front of Taihedian Hall (Hall of Supreme Harmony), where emperors ascended to the throne and met visiting officials.

33

ABOVE: Interior view of Taihedian Hall, the grandest hall in the Imperial Palace, from where the emperor ruled the country.

RIGHT: A bird's-eye view of the three front halls. From the left: Taihedian Hall; Zhonghedian Hall (Hall of Central Harmony); and Baohedian Hall (Hall of Preserving Harmony).

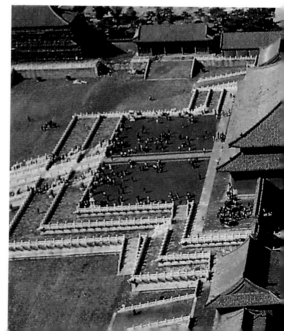

LEFT: This bronze lion guards the entrance to Taihedian Hall.

ABOVE: Wumen (Meridian) Gate is the most impressive in the Forbidden City. It is more than 115ft. high and has five openings.

RIGHT: This ornate ceiling in Taihedian Hall illustrates the lavish decoration of the Imperial Palace.

ABOVE AND RIGHT: Taihemen Gate. Note the five marble bridges spanning the Jinshuihe (Gold Water) Stream in the main picture.

FAR RIGHT: The bridal chamber in Kunninggong Palace (Palace of Terrestrial Tranquillity) was decorated in red to instill a warm and happy atmosphere.

ABOVE AND RIGHT: Views of Taihedian Hall. The bronze tortoise (RIGHT) symbolizes long life in Chinese culture.

FAR RIGHT: The Yujingting (Imperial View) Pavilion on Duixiu (Collecting Elegance) Hill. During the Qing Dynasty, every emperor would climb this hill to celebrate the Double Ninth Festival (held on the ninth day of the ninth lunar month) to escape misfortune.

PREVIOUS PAGES: The roofs of the Forbidden City. The building in the foreground is the Wumen Gate whose central arch was exclusively for the use of the emperor, although his empress was allowed to enter through this portal on her wedding day.

ABOVE: Qianqinggong Palace (Palace of Heavenly Purity) was built in 1420 and reconstructed in 1798.

RIGHT: Imperial steps on the northern side of Baohedian Hall were carved from Ming marble and enjoy the title "Dragon Pavement."

FAR RIGHT: An interior view of Taihedian Hall. The throne sits between two pillars decorated with dragons.

LEFT: Wanchunting (Everlasting Spring) Pavilion. There are five pavilions in the Imperial Gardens; each used to house a bronze statute of a god.

ABOVE: A painted ceiling in Yangxindian Hall. Emperor Dowager Longyu presided over the last Qing Dynasty cabinet meeting in this hall, before signing the formal Declaration of Abdication on February 12, 1912.

PREVIOUS PAGES: Full view of the Taihedian Hall facade. Due to its status as the symbol of Imperial power, no other building in the whole empire was permitted to be taller.

ABOVE: Changyinge Pavilion (the Belvedere of Flowing Music) is the largest theater at the Imperial Palace.

RIGHT: The Nine-Dragon Wall at Ningshougong Palace (Palace of Tranquil Longevity) was built in 1771 and is 11.5ft. high and 100ft. long.

FAR RIGHT: The eastern cabinet in Yangxindian Hall. It was from here that the Empress Dowager Cixi ruled China for forty-eight years.

LEFT: Sanxitang Hall (Hall of Three Rare Treasures), a small house at the west end of Yangxindian Hall.

RIGHT: The painted ceiling in Wanchunting Pavilion, the central pavilion which has three eaves and four upturned roof corners.

BELOW: Wumen (Meridian) Gate as seen from the Inner Jinshuihe Moat. Chinese emperors believed themselves to be the Sons of Heaven and that they should live at the center of the universe. In their view the Meridian Line passed through the Forbidden City, giving this gate its name.

ABOVE: Zhonghedian (which served as a private retreat for emperors) and Baohedian halls and the three-tier balustrades that surround them.

RIGHT: The back room of the eastern cabinet in the Yangxindian Hall.

LEFT: The Imperial Garden in the Forbidden City covers an area of almost 130,000sq ft.

LEFT: Alongside the steps ascending to Taihedian Hall, there are eighteen bronze dings (ancient Chinese vessels) that represented the number of national provinces at the time.

ABOVE: The Imperial throne in Taihedian Hall. It sits in front of a nine-dragon screen that symbolizes longevity and the unity of heaven and earth.

RIGHT: At each of the four corners of the Imperial Garden is a pavilion: they symbolize the four seasons.

PREVIOUS PAGES: Interior view of Taihedian Hall. The bricks used for the floor were fired and then polished by being soaked in tung oil—a drying oil made from pressed seed from tung tree nuts.

LEFT: Flank tower and moat at Wumen Gate. Although no longer occupied by royalty, the Imperial Palace remains a symbol of Chinese aristocracy.

RIGHT: Finial of Wanchunting Pavilion. It is possible to enjoy a 360-degree view of Beijing from this pavilion.

BELOW: The Hall of Preserving Harmony seen through the pillars of the Hall of Complete Harmony. The Hall of Preserving Harmony was used to hold the imperial examinations, the highest ranking civil service examinations.

THE MOGAO CAVES

THE MOGAO CAVES

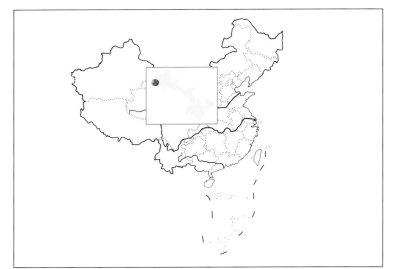

LOCATION: Cliffside of the eastern foot of Mingsha Mountain, Dunhuang City, Gansu Province.
REGISTERED: 1987 (cultural site).

The Mogao Caves are Buddhist cave-temples located in Gansu Province, at the eastern foot of Mingsha Mountain. They were carved out over a period of over a thousand years between the Sixteen States Period to Yuan times (317–1368 A.D.). Abandoned, they were lost for centuries until rediscovered in 1900 by a Taoist priest who chanced on a vault containing over 40,000 documents, handwritten scriptures, and cultural relics dating from different periods. All were miraculously still preserved in good condition—the discovery of the caves created a worldwide sensation.

Running north to south for almost three and a half miles the caves are cut high up on the cliff sides of Sanwei Hill. Here lie over 750 astonishing grottoes with walls covered by murals, more than 3,000 painted sculptures—including a 100ft. tall Buddha—and five wooden grotto eaves. The murals are so enormous that their combined height

LEFT: Buddhist monks valued austerity in life and hoped that these remote caves would aid their quest for enlightenment. The paintings helped meditation, and were also used to inform illiterate Chinese about Buddhist beliefs and stories. This painting from the Western Wei period (535–557 A.D.) shows bodhisattvas in the Heaven Palace.

ABOVE: Deva-musicians in the Heaven Palace as portrayed during the Northern Wei period (386–535 A.D.). Deva-musicians are dancers and musicians in the sky.

amounts to more than twenty miles; the subjects include scenes from the Jataka Tales, scenes from Buddhist sutras, Buddhist figures, and decorative designs.

In 139 and 119 B.C., Zhang Qian, envoy of the Han Dynasty, went to the west of China and opened up the Silk Road across continental Asia, stimulating cultural and economic exchanges between ancient China and the West. As an important hub of communication along the road, Dunhuang became a confluence of cultural streams from both East and West, and so rapidly attained great prosperity—indeed, the Chinese words "dun" and "huang" mean greatness and prosperity. It was through Dunhuang that Buddhism spread from the West into the interior of China.

The Mogao cave-temples reached their peak during the Sui and the early Tang periods and thrived until the decline of the Silk Road when Dunhuang fell into economic depression. No more grottoes were cut and the Mogao Caves were finally abandoned.

ABOVE, RIGHT AND FAR RIGHT: From the fourth to the fourteenth century, Buddhist monks at Dunhuang collected scriptures from the West, and many pilgrims passed through the area, painting murals inside the caves. Shown here are murals and sculptures from the Sui period (589–618 A.D.): colored sculptures (ABOVE); Deva-dancers and deva-musicians (RIGHT); and the head of Bodhisattva (FAR RIGHT). A bodhisattva is someone dedicated to helping others achieve Buddhahood. It is also used to mean the Buddha before he achieved enlightenment.

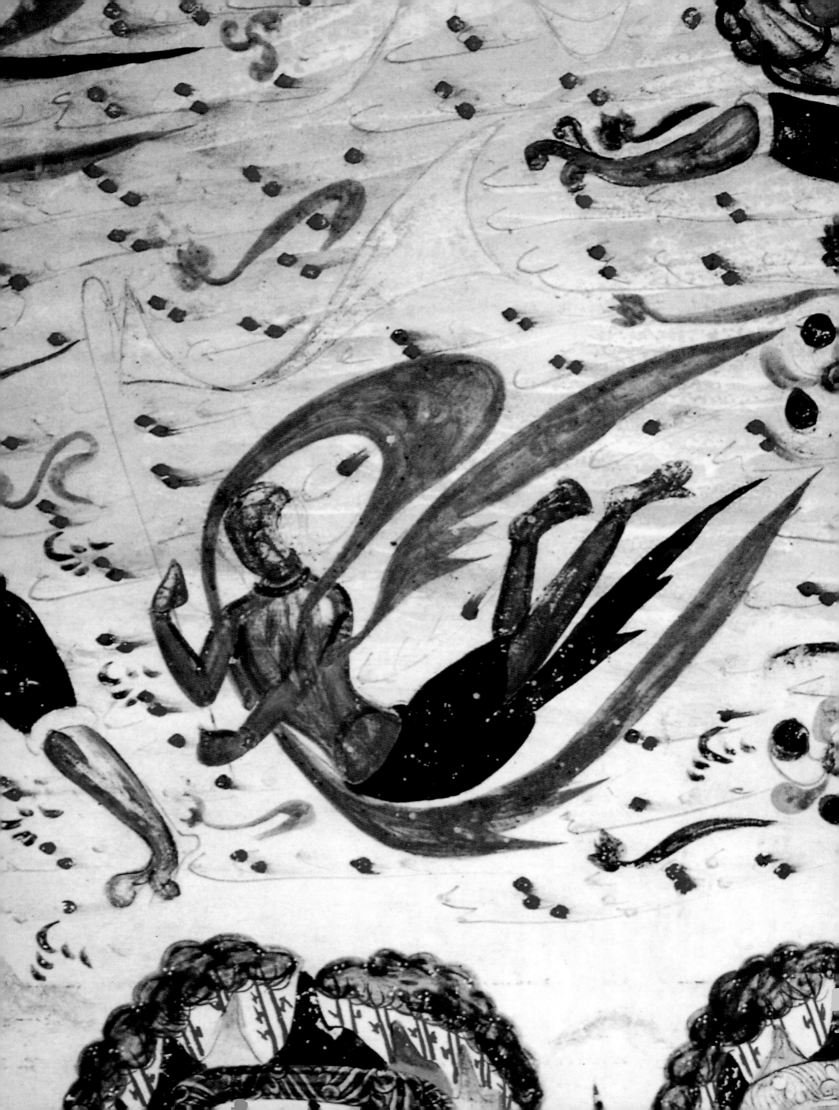

PREVIOUS PAGES: A Western Wei period mural depicting winged mythical animals and flying celestials.

ABOVE: Manjusri (Sui period) is the bodhisattva of keen awareness in Buddhism and represents wisdom, intelligence and realisation.

RIGHT: Kasyapa (Sui period) is an ancient sage and father of all humanity. His name means tortoise and he is connected to the cosmic tortoise.

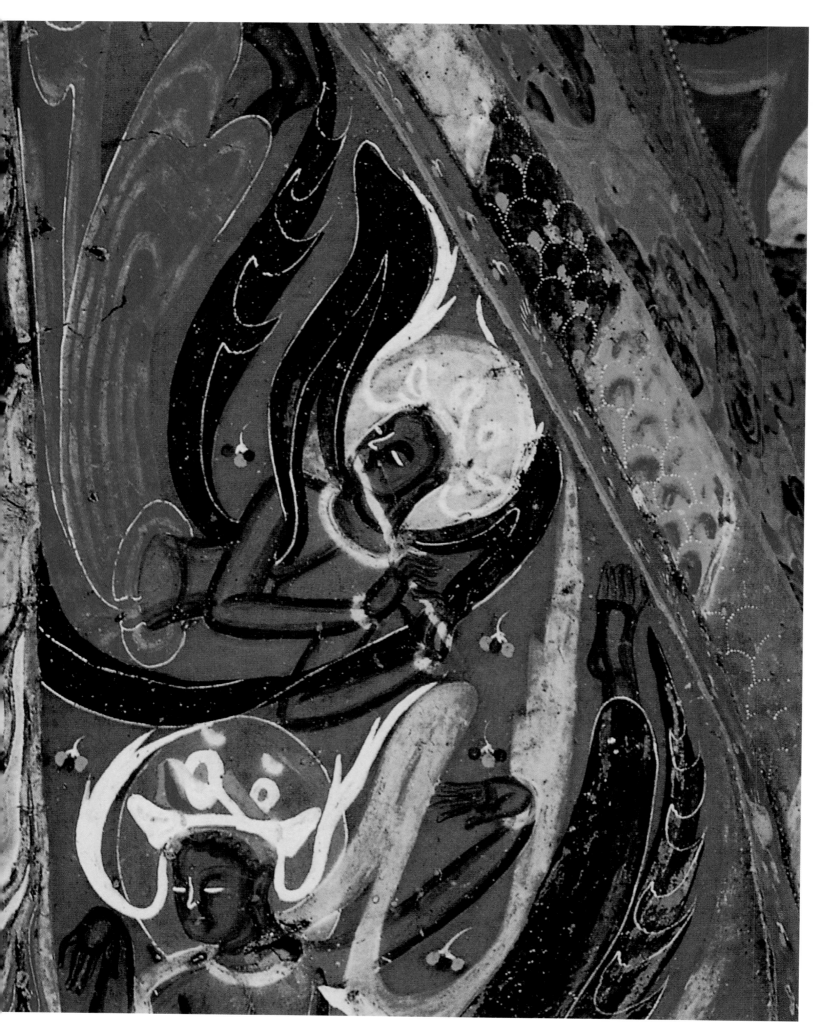

FAR LEFT: A close-up of a mural of deva-musicians from the Western Wei period.

LEFT AND BELOW LEFT: Two figures from the Tang period (618–907 A.D.): the head of Buddha and an attendant bodhisattva.

LEFT: The painted sculptures that form a large part of the treasures of the Mogao Caves were created over a period spanning a thousand years.

ABOVE: Scene from the Jataka story of Sattva, Northern Zhou period (557–589 A.D.). The Jakata is a body of folklore and mythic literature concerned with previous births of the Buddha. Some people believe that they formed the basis for Aesop's Fables, Sindbad the Sailor, and The Arabian Nights.

RIGHT: An attendant bodhisattva from the Tang period.

LEFT: Bodhisattvas, Tang period. A Bodhisattva is a Buddha-to-be who delays entry into nibbana (nirvana) to help other beings out of suffering. Bodhisattvas are said to go through ten stages or bhumis.

RIGHT: Entering into conception on an elephant, Sui period. According to belief, Buddha's mother, Maya, had a dream after twenty years of sterility in which she saw an elephant entering into her womb through the right side of her chest, and so she became pregnant.

BELOW: Sakyamuni (one of the pseudonyms of Gautama Buddha) and Prabhutaratna—a Buddha from the Lotus Sutra—as depicted in this Western Wei period image.

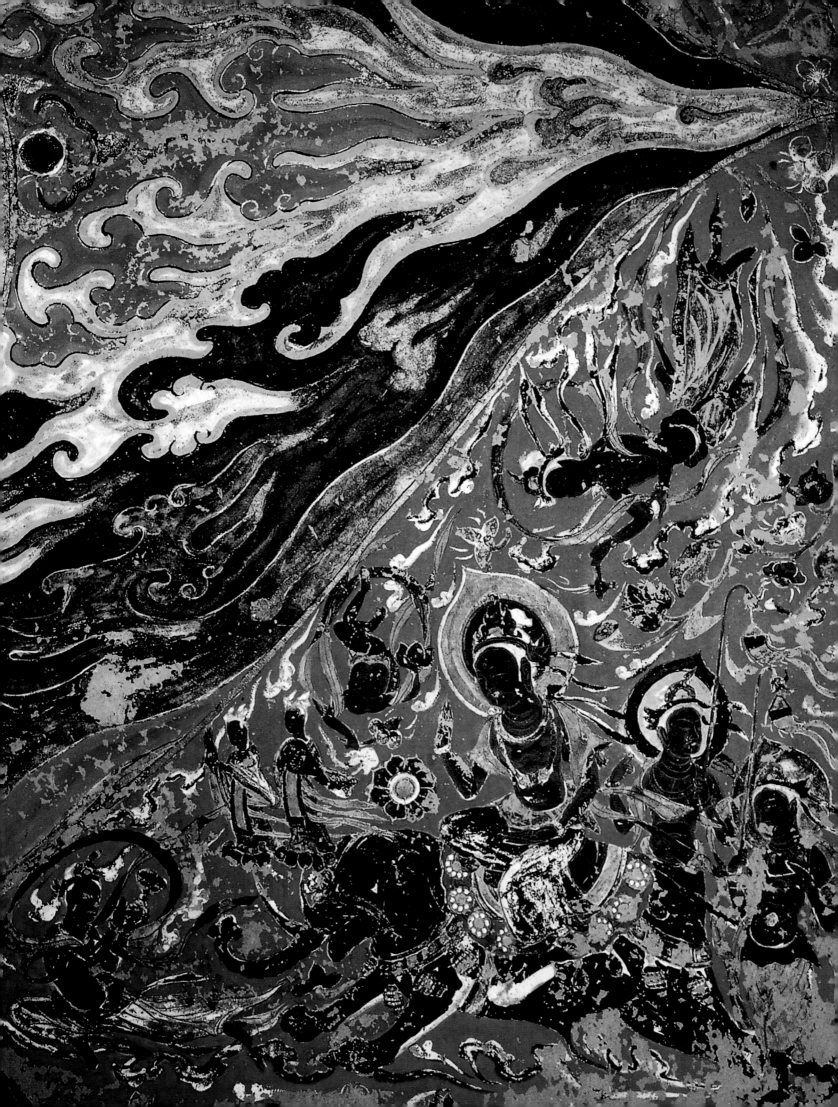

FAR LEFT, LEFT AND PAGES 80–81: More images from the Tang period. Deva-musicians, mid-Tang period (FAR LEFT); Bodhisattva (LEFT); and a Quadriga, high-Tang period (PAGES 80–81).

BELOW: "Five Hundred Bandits Becoming Buddhas": Fighting, Western Wei period.

LEFT: Cave 156 with its Procession of Zhang Yichao and his troops, late-Tang period, was completed in 865 A.D.

BELOW LEFT: "Five Hundred Bandits Becoming Buddhas": Hunting, Western Wei period.

BELOW: The main hall of Cave 432 houses a statue of a sitting Buddha and, on either side outside the niche, is a bodhisattva statue.

MAUSOLEUM OF THE FIRST QIN EMPEROR AND TERRA-COTTA WARRIORS

MAUSOLEUM OF THE FIRST QIN EMPEROR AND TERRA-COTTA WARRIORS

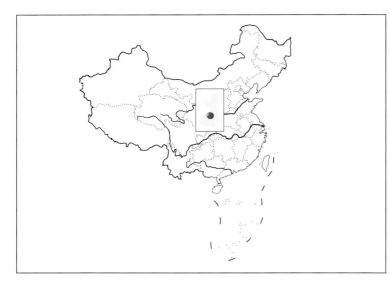

The Terra-cotta Army of Emperor Qin discovered in the early 1970s in Lintong County, Shaanxi Province is one of the most astonishing archeological finds of the twentieth century. So far the painstaking excavations have revealed funeral objects and over eight hundred terra-cotta warriors, a hundred terra-cotta horses, and eighteen wooden chariots.

PREVIOUS PAGES: Warriors and horses at Qin Shi Huang's Mausoleum. Local peasants found pottery while digging a well nearby in 1974.

BELOW: Qin Shi Huang—first Emperor of a unified China between 221 and 210 B.C.—stipulated that lifesize clay soldiers should protect him in the afterlife.

RIGHT: Part of a terra-cotta vanguard. The figures were sculpted out of local clay and kilns were established in the neighboring Shangjiao, Yuchi, and Chengou villages.

LOCATION: Northern foot of Lishan Hill in Lintong District, Xi'an City, Shaanxi Province.

REGISTERED: 1987 (cultural site).

ABOVE: No. 1 terra-cotta warriors and horses pit—at 153,493 square feet it is the largest of the three pits.

BELOW: Terra-cotta figures of soldiers and infantrymen. The upper body section of the figures is hollow, as can be seen on the left.

RIGHT: A close-up of the head of one of the many terra-cotta officers. Facial features were created by use of a mold.

LEFT: This bronze carriage was unearthed from the precincts of Qin Shi Huang's Mausoleum in December 1980.

RIGHT: A second bronze carriage was discovered at the same time. Here the driver is still being excavated from the surrounding soil.

BELOW: Bronze horses and carriage unearthed from the mausoleum. The models on these pages are the largest delicate bronze pieces that have been found anywhere in the world.

RIGHT: Head of a terra-cotta warrior. Although the colors have deteriorated over the last 2,000 years, it is obvious how impressive these figures would have looked.

BELOW RIGHT: More terra-cotta warriors and horses. Each of the warriors would have carried a bronze weapon such as a sword, dagger, spear or crossbow.

FAR RIGHT: Bronze horses being excavated. The horses would have pulled a half-size scale model of a real chariot of the period.

PEKING MAN SITE

PEKING MAN SITE

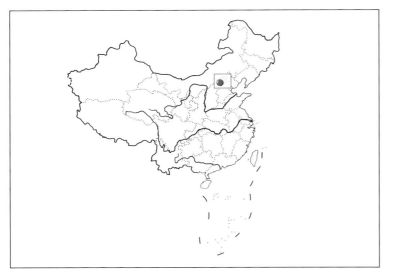

LOCATION: Longgu (Dragon Bone) Hill at
            Zhoukoudian, Fangshan District, Beijing.
REGISTERED: 1987 (cultural site).

PREVIOUS PAGES: A general view of the Peking Man site at Zhoukoudian, a small village some thirty miles southwest of Beijing.

BELOW: The first discovered intact skullcap of Peking Man. Although this and the other fossils disappeared in the 1940s, the search has continued and a total of six skullcaps have now been unearthed.

The Peking Man cave-site was discovered in 1921 on the northern side of Dragon Bone Hill at Zhoukoudian. It contains the most abundant remains of Palaeolithic man recorded so far. To date, fossils of around forty individuals have been discovered, along with thousands of stone tools, ornaments, numerous bones, antler artifacts, and fire remains.

The discovery of human fossil teeth gave birth to the name "*Sinanthropus pekinensis.*" Then, in 1929, a fossil skullcap was brought to light from the site along with man-made stone implements. The skull is quite primitive, but possesses features characteristic of the modern Mongoloid.

The cultural deposits in the cave cover a period between roughly 700,000 and 230,000 years B.C., suggesting that Peking Man lived there for nearly five hundred millennia. Peking Man was primarily a hunter-gatherer and knew how to use fire for cooking because substantial fire remains have been found.

RIGHT: Interior view of the Peking Man site that was one of the first in China to enter UNESCO's World Heritage List. It redefined popular thinking as to how early man used fire as a tool.

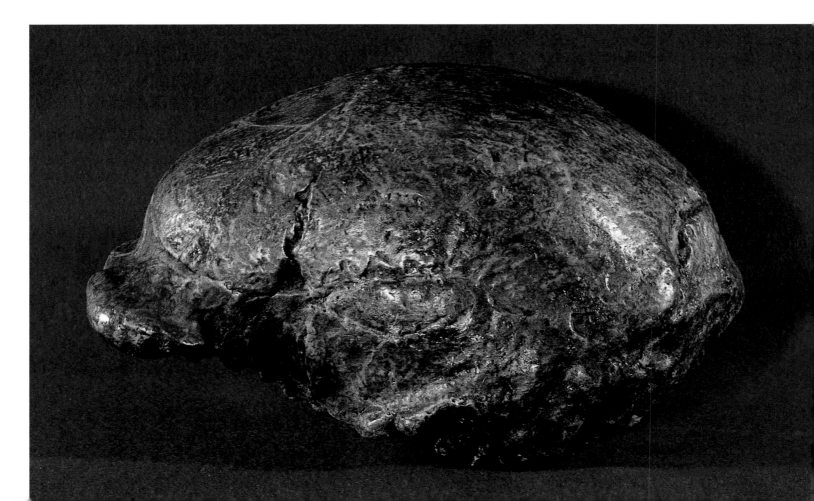

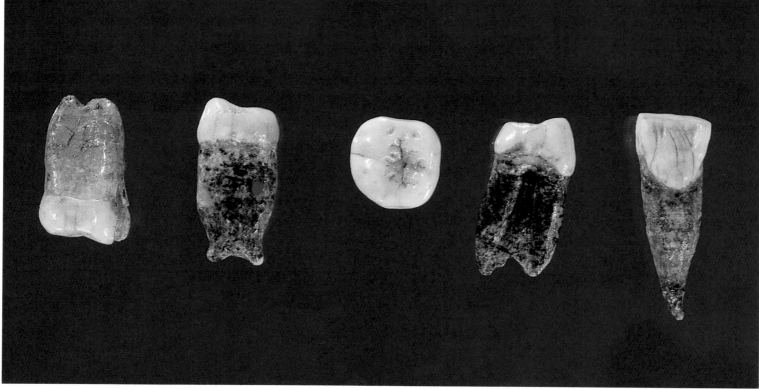

TOP: Exterior view of the Peking Man Site Exhibition Center which is divided into seven display rooms.

ABOVE: Fossil teeth of Peking Man. Remains discovered indicate that 70 percent died before age 14 while fewer than five percent reached 50.

RIGHT: An artist's interpretation of how Peking Man would have looked, based on the fossils unearthed.

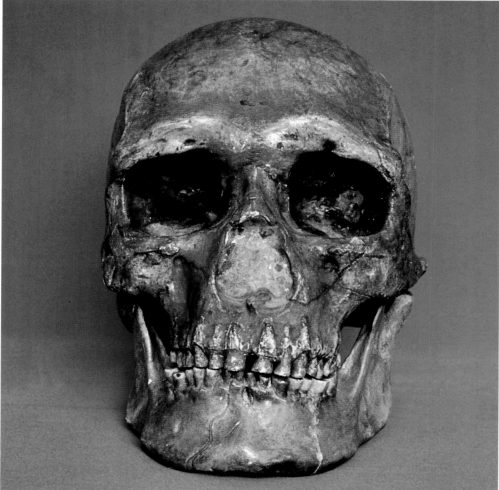

ABOVE: Artist's impression of how Peking Man engaged in gathering food. Their society lived in the limestone caves and survived by hunting and gathering.

ABOVE RIGHT: Exterior view of the Upper Cave Man site, at an altitude of 410ft., that was first excavated in the 1930s.

RIGHT: More than 140 ornaments belonging to Upper Cave Man have been discovered.

LEFT: The skull of Upper Cave Man, who lived in the area around 27,000 years ago.

MOUNT TAISHAN

MOUNT TAISHAN

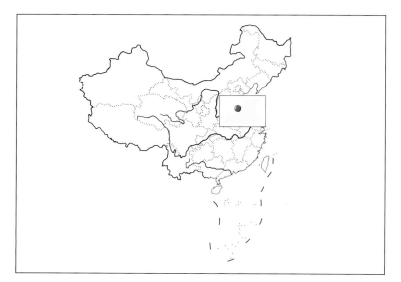

LOCATION: Central Shandong Province.
REGISTERED: 1987 (mixed cultural and natural site).

Mount Taishan is the most important of China's "Five Sacred Mountains." Also named "Dongyue" or Mountain of the East, it is associated with sunrise, birth, and renewal. Prominent on the vast North China Plain in Shandong Province, Mount Tai rises 5,000ft above sea level to its highest point— Yuhuangding (Jade Emperor Peak), at 5,068ft. The Taishan massif is an imposing and substantial area of 165 square miles: "as steady as Taishan" is a popular Chinese saying in reference to its vast size; "If Mount Tai is stable, so is the entire country," runs another.

There are traces of human activity around the Taishan region as early as 400,000 years ago during the Paleolithic period, but it was not until about 50–60,000 years ago that people began to worship Taishan itself. Over time, this worship evolved into an official imperial rite and Mount Tai became one of the principal places where the emperor

PREVIOUS PAGES: Side view of Bixia (Azure Cloud) Temple atop Mount Taishan—a combination of metal components, wood, brick, and stone structures—dedicated to the daughter of the God of Mount Tai.

LEFT: One of the many inscriptions on a Mount Taishan cliffside. Many famous poets and scholars visited this area for inspiration and it also played a role in the development of Buddhism and Taoism.

ABOVE: An overall view of the Eighteen-Bend Steps. On accession, each of the ancient emperors had to climb Mount Taishan and pray to heaven and earth for their ancestors.

would pay homage to Heaven (on the summit) and Earth (at the foot of the mountain) in the Fengshan Sacrifices. According to ancient records from the Pre-Qin Dynasty, seventy-two rulers came to Mount Taishan to officiate in the worship of Heaven and Earth. The First Emperor of the Qin Dynasty, Qin Shi Huang, held a ceremony on the summit in 219 B.C. and proclaimed the unity of his empire in a famous inscription. Other important emperors such as Hu Hai, the second emperor, and Emperor Wudi of the Han Dynasty, officiated at the rites here. The veneration continued through the Song and Ming dynasties until in the reign of Kangxi and Qianlong of the Qing Dynasty Taishan was raised to the holiest stature.

Taishan attracted scholars, calligraphers, and artists who left behind a large quantity of immortal works including famous essays, rock inscriptions, and stone tablets. In the Northern Qi Dynasty the Diamond Sutra was carved in the Sutra Rock Valley. Many historic buildings and 1,800 stone inscriptions are still preserved here.

LEFT: Autumnal trees on Zhongxi Mountain. Some of the trees in the Mount Taishan area date back 2,100 years.

TOP: The impressive archway at the Yaocan Pavilion, Dai Temple (Temple of the God of Mount Tai).

ABOVE: Pool of the Queen Mother at the Temple of the Heavenly Dowager at the base of the mountain.

FAR LEFT: The Heaven-Bestowed Hall in the Dai Temple, the largest and most complete ancient building complex in the area.

LEFT: Daimiao (Dai Temple) Arch. The temple was first built in the Qin Dynasty and occupies a vast area.

BELOW: This is Jade Emperor Peak, the highest point on Mount Taishan, at a height of 5,068ft. The Jade Emperor became the patron saint of the Imperial family during the ninth century B.C.

TOP: The Imperial Stele Pavilion in the Dai Temple. While the original site dates back over 2,200 years, several dynasties have left their unique style.

RIGHT: One of the sights most associated with Mount Taishan, the 500-plus year old Guest-Expecting Pine.

FAR RIGHT: Mount Taishan is known as the most important of the "Five Sacred Mountains" and attracts millions of visitors each year.

MOUNT HUANGSHAN

MOUNT HUANGSHAN

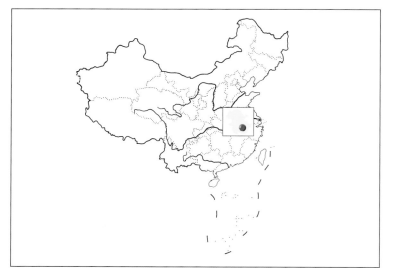

LOCATION: Southern Anhui Province.
REGISTERED: 1990 (Mixed cultural and natural site).

The Huangshan mountain range is an area of great natural beauty in southern Anhui Province. It is justly famous for its scenery—its strangely jutting granite peaks, many of which are well over 5,000ft., and its weather-shaped pine trees. Over ten thousand pines grow around Huangshan's slopes, many of them over a hundred years old, and individually named.

The Huangshan Pine (*Pinus hwangshanensis*) is native to much of eastern China although named specifically after Huangshan. Reaching 75ft. or more in height, it grows at surprisingly high altitudes, where the weather shapes the trees into extraordinary, lovely forms, much loved by Chinese painters, poets, and artists over the centuries.

The Huangshan landscape is unique, with one peak rising after another between ever-changing mists and clouds. The tallest peaks in the range are Lotus Flower

PREVIOUS PAGES: "The Monkey Gazing at the Sea," one of the picturesque sights of Mount Huangshan. Originally known as Mount Yishan, it was renamed in 747 A.D. in honor of the alleged ancestor of the Chinese people, Huang Di.

LEFT: The breathtaking view of the Huangshan range are enhanced by the unpredictable mists and clouds, that swirl among the majestic peaks on more than 200 days each year.

ABOVE: The pine trees on the mountain have grown in fascinating shapes and many have been named, such as See-Guest-Off Pine and, here, Guest-Expecting Pine.

Peak, which rises to 6,115ft. above sea level, Bright Summit Peak (6,036ft.), and Celestial Peak (6,000ft.) but there are seventy-seven peaks over 3,250ft. In addition there are stone forests, pillars, waterfalls, and deep pools. The mountain is crisscrossed with ancient paths and stone steps that link up the various beauty spots and historic locations.

Mount Huangshan has a long history as a mountain of culture. According to legend, Emperor Xuanyuan—the early ancestor of the Chinese nation—succeeded in his quest to discover a potion for the secret of eternal life in here. Having found the way, Xuanyuan ascended to Heaven with his elixir. This brought good fortune and beautiful natural scenery to Huangshan. Throughout the ages, Chinese scholars, philosophers, poets, and artists, have been attracted to Huangshan; between the time of the Tang Dynasty and the late Qing Dynasty hundreds of essays and over 20,000 poems have been written on Huangshan in praise of the mountain. In particular, the Huangshan school of painting is a prime example of the long history of traditional Chinese painting.

ABOVE: Celestial-Capital (meaning capital of the immortals and city of heaven) Peak is the steepest of the three major peaks and reaches 6,000ft.

ABOVE: The "Stone Parlor" on Tiandu (Celestial-Capital) Peak—note the stone steps cut into the rock; there are thousand such steps all over the range. Not visible in this picture, Celestial Peak's summit is flat with a cave large enough to hold 100 people.

LEFT: Although Huangshan is famous for its oddly shaped pine trees, below an altitude of 3,000ft. the trees are more uniform. This is called "Pines in Love."

ABOVE: The magnificent Jade Screen Peak in fall. A hotel now offers guests welcome respite and outstanding views on the site where a temple used to exist.

LEFT: In 2002, Mount Huangshan became sister mountain to Mount Jungfrau, another World Heritage site, in Switzerland. Here we see "Three Islets in the Wonderland."

ABOVE: Several waterfalls enhance the mountainous landscape with their cascading beauty. This one is called "White Dragon Soaring to the Sky."

LEFT: The inscription carved on Standing Horse
Peak reads "look ahead to Dong Hai and Tai Ping
at the top of Standing Horse Peak."

ABOVE: Probably the most famous tree in the area,
Guest-Welcoming Pine is reported to be over
1,500 years old.

JIUZHAIGOU VALLEY SCENIC AND HISTORIC INTEREST AREA

JIUZHAIGOU VALLEY SCENIC AND HISTORY INTEREST AREA

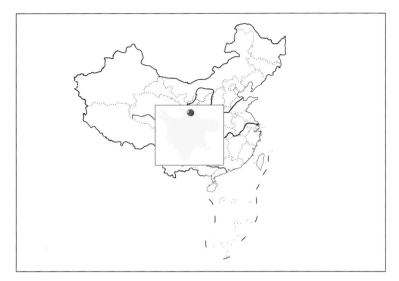

LOCATION: Nanping County, Aba Tibetan and Qiang Autonomous Prefecture, Sichuan Province.
REGISTERED: 1992 (natural site).

Jiuzhaigou is regarded by local Tibetans as "a land of divine mountains and holy waters." Here the magnificent snowy mountains tower well over 13,000ft and live side by side with charming brooks and streams. The fantastic scenery is mainly composed of high mountains, highland calcareous tufa shoals, pure and transparent lakes, dense forests, waterfalls, babbling brooks, and rapids, as well as its unique Tibetan customs.

The main Jiuzhaigou valley is more than thirty miles long and consists of three principal gullies that form a "Y" shape. Altogether there are 114 lakes, 17 groups of waterfalls, 5 calcareous tufa shoals, 47 springs, and 11 rapid streams filled with icy cold but clear water. With an altitude difference of well over three thousand feet they plunge through the snow-clad mountain peaks, forests, and gullies for thirty miles.

Jiuzhaigou is situated in a zone where the Qinghai-Tibet Plateau slopes down to the Sichuan Basin. The geological structure is complicated with a wide distribution of carbonate rocks, splitting and transforming into folds to create this spectacular landscape. Due to the strong upward

PREVIOUS PAGES: Jiuzhaigou Valley means Valley of Nine Villages—but few of the original Tibetan villages survive today. The main feature of the area is its Karst topography and its brightly colored lakes.

LEFT: Shuzheng Waterfall, one of the biggest and most impressive waterfalls in the Jiuzhaigou Valley, is a beautiful multitiered waterfall that empties into Shuzheng Lake.

ABOVE: Chang Hai (Long Lake) is the largest lake in Jiuzhaigou and sits at more than 9,800ft. above seal level. The S-shaped lake is nearly 2.5 miles long and up to 250ft. deep.

movement of the Earth's crust and other tectonic forces, the valley has developed a variety of landforms. Mountains with heights between 13,000ft and nearly 18,000ft cover a third of the total area and the remains of the glaciers formed in the Quaternary Period are the best preserved in China.

Due to the great difference in mountain height, the vertical distribution of plants is distinct; there are more than 2,000 different plants. There are seventeen species of rare animals, among which the giant panda, ox-antelope, and golden monkey are designated as first-class state-protected animals.

ABOVE: Jiuzhaigou mountain scenery. There are fifteen different species of rhododendron to be found in this area.

RIGHT: Nuorilang (meaning magnificent in Tibetan) Ice Fall. At other times of the year, this is a 300ft.-wide cascade of water.

PAGES 134–135: The impressive Pearl Beach Waterfall drops about 100ft. Above the waterfall, there is a fan-shaped calcium mesa.

FAR LEFT: Jiuzhaigou is best known for its dozens of clear blue, green, and turquoise lakes.

ABOVE AND LEFT: Part of a group of forty lakes and waterfalls in the area, Shuzheng Lake and Waterfall—in the shadow of Dege Mountain—are close to Shuzheng Stockade, a typical Tibetan village.

OPPOSITE, ABOVE: Lying-Dragon Lake. The calcareous dyke, palely visible from the surface, looks like a sleeping dragon.

OPPOSITE, BELOW: A full view of Nuorilang. According to legend, the goddess Wonosmo dropped a mystical mirror that broke to become the lakes.

LEFT: Immense forests cover the slopes and include two types of bamboo critical for the survival of the giant panda.

HUANGLONG SCENIC AND HISTORIC AREA

HUANGLONG SCENIC AND HISTORIC INTEREST AREA

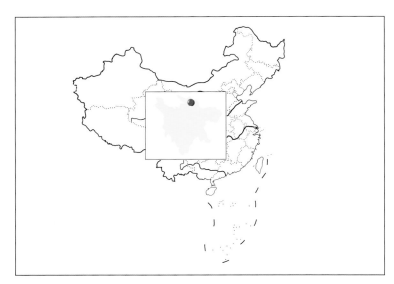

LOCATION: Songpan County Aba Tibetan and Qiang Autonomous Prefecture, Sichuan Province.

REGISTERED: 1992 (natural site).

Huanglong is known for its colorful pools, snow-covered mountains, deep gorges, and dense forests. Travertine—concreted limestone—deposits at the mouth of hot springs wind their way like golden dragons through the virgin forest between the rocky icy peaks where they form truly bizarre, perilous, and wild environmental features.

Huanglong owes its unique topography to its position at the meeting point of three major geotectonic units: the Yangtze quasi-platform, the Songpan-Garze fold system, and the Qinling fold system. Because of this, the region's geography is complex and in a continuous (in geological terms) state of transition.

The main attraction is Huanglong's huge travertine formations, which are remarkable for their size and color, exquisite structure, primeval appearance, and great variety. There are travertine ponds, lakes, springs, terraces, fans, waterfalls, caverns, and miniature landscapes. Combined,

PREVIOUS PAGES: Colorful pools with the reflection of the Fairy Hills. The Huanglong area is famous for its travertine (calcium carbonate) formations that are scattered all around the valley.

LEFT: Erdaohai Lake in late fall. This body of water is sacred to the Tibetans and they visit the lake each spring to worship. There are numerous underground limestone caverns around the lake.

ABOVE: Seercuo Hotel, built with Tibetan architecture in mind, has 300 beds. Six miles of roads and bridges have been constructed in the area to accommodate the number of tourists wishing to visit.

these formations are well over two miles in length—the longest is four-fifths of a mile long—and there are as many as 3,400 colorful ponds. The famous Zhaga waterfall is 328ft. from top to bottom.

Additionally the area has numerous precious species of flora and fauna; many of the 1,500 plants are rare species. While the rare giant panda, golden monkey, takin, Yunnan leopard, white-lipped deer, Temminck's tragopan (a type of pheasant), and white-eared pheasant are all endangered and state-protected animals.

ABOVE: Xuebaoding (Snow Treasure Peak) is snow-capped all year and rises to an altitude of more than 18,000ft. It is also boasts ancient glaciers.

RIGHT: The spectacular Annular Waterfall. The water that flows through this valley is said to be able to cure infertility and possess healing qualities.

PREVIOUS PAGES: The color of each of the many pools is dictated by the amount of calcium bicarbonate in the water.

LEFT: A calcareous tufa waterfall. Wildlife thrives in the region, home to rare species like giant panda and Sichuan golden snub-nosed monkey.

ABOVE: Dragon-Hiding Mountain. This scenic and historic interest area encompasses both the Huanglong and Muni valleys.

RIGHT: The biggest tufa formation in the valley is the 4,265ft. long Jinsha Pudi (Golden Sand Beach).

FAR RIGHT: The yellow in these colorful pools gave Huanglong (Yellow Dragon) Valley its name.

LEFT: Zhaga Waterfall, over 300ft. high and 100ft. wide, is one of the main attractions of this area.

TOP: Gongga Mountain, the highest peak of Daxue Mountain, at the fountainhead of the Minjiang River.

ABOVE: Looking like liquid rock, this calcite stream is typical of the area.

WULINGYUAN SCENIC AND HISTORIC INTEREST AREA

WULINGYUAN SCENIC AND HISTORIC INTEREST AREA

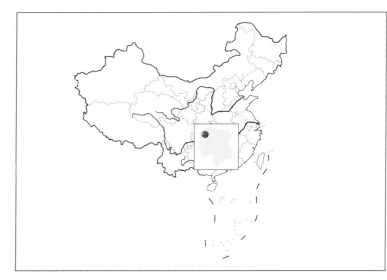

LOCATION: Zhangjiajie City, Hunan Province.
REGISTERED: 1992 (natural site).

Wulingyuan is famous for its remarkable karst formations. The area contains over three thousand exotically shaped quartz sandstone peaks which make a beautiful and unique landscape that also includes odd-looking stones, deep and secluded ravines, beautiful waters, and karst caves. There are dense forests, colorful springs and streams, and ever-changing mists and clouds.

Away from the peaks the scenery is more graceful—farmland with streams flowing through it. The terrain ascends gradually up to meet the peaks over fields that are dotted with cottages and surrounded by green trees and bamboo groves. Smoke rises from the chimneys.

The quartz sandstone peaks of Wulingyuan are incomparable; as you stand on the high platform of the Tianzishan (Son of Heaven Peak) or Huangshizhai (Yellow

PREVIOUS PAGES: "Grand Peak Forest" at Wulingyuan. This fascinating formation was created by long-term erosion caused by the action of surface water and groundwater. The water flowed through and encroached on the quartzite, which formed in the Devonian Period of the Paleozoic Era.

LEFT: Sea of clouds at Tianzi (Son of Heaven) Peak. Local legends say that an ancient Tujia chieftain who aspired to become the Son of Heaven, gathered his people and launched an uprising from this peak.

ABOVE: Trysters Peaks, part of a large forest of natural peaks on the thick quartz and sandstone base. Many rocks are shaped like animals and fairies, and most have been given their own legends.

Stone Village) you'll overlook a densely wooded landscape of various size peaks, some fantastic, others grotesque, but mostly lofty and elegant. Camel Peak, for instance, is shaped exactly like a camel, with head, neck, and tail clearly visible; the hump is particularly lifelike. Meanwhile, the jagged Drunken Stone Peak is bigger at the top than the bottom,

and although straight and upright in shape its body slopes to the south at an angle of ninetee degrees. Standing below it, you think it is about to fall on your head.

The Wulingyuan protected area covers a hundred square miles within which grows a remarkable primeval botanical community, particularly along the Yangtze River valley where the ancient flora remains intact. Here lives the ancient gingko tree, over 160ft. tall and 5ft. in diameter, and accurately described as a living fossil. There are also rare species such as the dove tree, yew, *Bretschneidera sinensis*, and spicebush. The local tree, the Wuling pine is distributed over an extensive area and so well preserved that it has come to be called "hundred and eighty thousand pine"—a reference to its great numbers.

Wulingyuan also has some thirteen species of rare animals which have important scientific value, especially for the study of the relationship between wild animals and the local ecological system.

157

ABOVE: Bamboo-Shoot Peaks, grotesque and yet elegant. There are over 1,000 peaks which rise at least 650ft.

RIGHT: "Fields in the Air," part of the system of streams, brooks, springs, lakes, and waterfalls that make the area so spectacular.

LEFT: Celestial Pillar Peak, part of an inaccessible area that remained untouched until after the People's Republic of China was formed in 1949.

ABOVE: Suoxi Brook winds for around forty miles through the site; in fall, it is one of the primary features in the area.

LEFT: Seven-Maiden Peak (in the distance). About three billion and eight thousand years ago, this place was covered by a large patch of ocean.

ABOVE: A view of the Jinbianxi (Golden Whip) Brook, one of the many watercourses running through the area.

163

LEFT: One of two spectacular natural bridges in the area: Xianren Qiao or "Bridge of the Immortals" is 85ft. long and over 300ft. above the gorge.

BELOW: Between Wulingyuan's 3,103 karst peaks lie ravines and gorges—often obscured by mist or low-lying cloud.

THE MOUNTAIN RESORT AT CHENGDE AND OUTLYING TEMPLES

THE MOUNTAIN RESORT AT CHENGDE AND OUTLYING TEMPLES

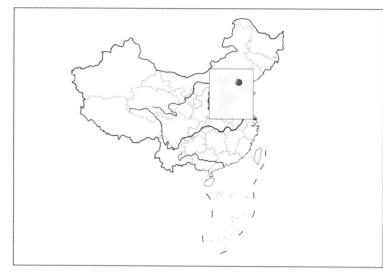

LOCATION: Chengde City, Hebei Province.
REGISTERED: 1994 (cultural site).

Emperor Kangxi of the Qing Dynasty decided that Chengde in Hebei Province was the ideal site for a palace on account of its excellent topography, beautiful landscape, and congenial weather. It was also well-placed politically, to promote his home region in Northeast China, to help consolidate his rule over the Guannei or "China within the Great Wall," and close enough to the border to control the various tribes in Mongolia.

Chengde is contained in a long and narrow valley on the west bank of the Wulie River. Emperor Kangxi used to hunt here while he made his annual North China tour. To improve his travels he built many palaces along his regular routes and Bishushanzhuang—or "Mountain Manor to Escape the Summer Heat" as the palace is called—is the largest of them.

PREVIOUS PAGES: Aerial view of Putuo Zongcheng Temple. Built in 1771 to celebrate the Emperor Qianlong's birthday, this temple is similar to the Potala Palace in Lhasa.

LEFT: Zhijing Yundi Dyke as seen from the Shuixin (Mid-lake) Pavilion, located between Xia Lake and Silver Lake. The pavilion forms part of the official tourist symbol for Chengde City.

ABOVE: The imposing entrance to Putuo Zongcheng Temple. Known as the Lesser Potala Palace, this temple covers an area of just over fifty acres and was used to host important religious ceremonies.

Building began in 1703 (the forty-second year of Kangxi's reign) with the dredging of lakes, road building, house construction—and most importantly, a massive series of imperial gardens and parks. Thirty-six scenic spots (the Kangxi 36 Scenes) with enclosed walls were completed by 1713. Construction was halted during the reign of Yongzheng but began again in 1741 under Emperor

Qianlong. The palace was finally completed in 1792; in all, construction had taken nearly ninety years.

Later additions—some thirty-six scenes of Qianlong plus eight religious shrines on the outskirts of the resort—increased the area to around fifty acres. The palace is built against mountains towering over lakes and its gardens incorporate nature into their design.

There are four scenic areas based on the topography: the palace area is on the southern bank of the lake near the city, convenient for the emperors to attend to administrative affairs. The lake district, north of the palace, is dotted with eight islands, dividing the district into eight sections, modeled after scenic places among the waters of South China. North of the lake the vast grassland plain at the foot of the mountain contains Wanmuyuan (Ten Thousand Tree Orchard) and Shimadai (Flatland to Run Horses during Training). The hilly area is northwest of the villa and occupies about four-fifths of the area.

LEFT: The Snow Drifts Pavilion on South Hill. The shortest river in the world—the Rehe (Jehol) at only nine miles long—runs through the resort.

RIGHT: The Grand Platform in Pule (Temple of Universal Joy) Temple. Built in 1766, Xuguan Pavilion was styled on Beijing's Temple of Heaven.

BELOW: Full view of the Mid-lake Pavilion which was fully restored in 1998.

LEFT: Hall of the Wind in the Pines of Ten Thousand River Valleys (Wanhesongfengdian) was built for Emperor Kangxi to receive officials.

ABOVE: Upper Lake as seen from the God Pavilion. It is one of a group of lakes known collectively as the Frontier (Sai) Lakes.

PREVIOUS PAGES: Yanyu House (House of Mists and Rains) on the Qinglian (Green Lotus Islet) is a copy of a tower at Jiaxing City.

LEFT: An eastern view seen from the Beizhen Shuangfeng Pavilion at the Mountain Resort, China's largest existing imperial garden.

BELOW: Niches on the Great Red Platform in Putuo Zongcheng Temple. The tops of its three halls are covered with copper gold tiles.

ABOVE: Linfang Villa is laid out around a square courtyard in the typical style of northern China, each hall connected to the next by a roofed corridor.

RIGHT: Full view of Puning Temple, built in 1755. It boasts the world's largest woodcarving of Buddha at 73ft. high and 50ft. wide.

LEFT: The palace wall of the Mountain Resort is over six miles long and winds its way through plains and high mountains like the Great Wall.

RIGHT: The Water Chestnuts Gathering Ferry. Many of the buildings in the resort were constructed with the emperor's safety in mind. For example, a concealed door was installed behind the bed in his sleeping quarters—the Hall of Cool Mists and Ripples (Yanbozhishuangdian)— offering a means of escape.

FAR RIGHT: Painted ceiling in the Rising Sun Light Pavilion in Pule Temple. Much of the temple was built with wood blocks called Stramonium. There are seventy-two woods symbolizing the seventy-two kinds of wisdom of Buddha.

BELOW: Golden finial of the Miaogao Zhuangyan Hall in the Felicity and Longevity Sumeru Temple.

PREVIOUS PAGES: The Mahayana Pavilion in Puning Temple was built in 1755.

LEFT: The Auspicious Hall in the Felicity and Longevity Sumeru Temple, styled on the Tashilhunpo Monastery.

RIGHT: The Five-Pagoda Gate, built in 1768, and stone elephant in Putuo Zongcheng Temple. According to Buddhist scripture, Buddhist monks and devotees should pass through the gateway at least twice a day to show their respect for and devotion to Buddha.

BELOW: On the summit of Golden Hill (on the shores of Clear Lake) stands the Pavilion of the Supreme Emperor (Shangdige), a three-story hexagonal building which originally served as a temple for the worship of two Daoist gods: Immortal Wu Di and the Jade Emperor.

TEMPLE AND CEMETERY OF CONFUCIUS AND THE KONG FAMILY MANSION

TEMPLE AND CEMETERY OF CONFUCIUS AND THE KONG FAMILY MANSION

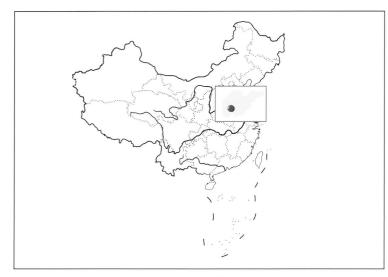

LOCATION: Qufu City, Shandong Province.
REGISTERED: 1994 (cultural site).

The temple and cemetery of Confucius and the Kong family mansion are in Qufu City, Shandong Province. They form a large complex and contain the temple for offering sacrifices to Confucius; the mansion where his direct descendants live; and the cemetery containing the remains of Confucius and his descendants.

Confucius (551–479 B.C.) was a philosopher whose teachings led to a school of thought that became adopted as the Chinese state religion. From the Han Dynasty (206 B.C.–220 A.D.), Chinese emperors revered Confucius and promoted the study of his thoughts. Two years after his death, his home was converted into the Confucius Temple, where offerings were made to him every year. Posthumous titles were regularly given to Confucius and his temple was enlarged many times. The present Temple sits in fifty-four acres and contains 466 buildings and nine courtyards.

PREVIOUS PAGES: Dacheng Hall (Hall of Great Accomplishment) is the main building in the temple, where the memorial ceremony for Confucius was often held.

LEFT: The tomb of Confucius. The original tomb erected here had the shape of an axe with a brick platform for sacrifices. The present-day tomb is a cone-shaped hill. When it was opened by Red Guards during the Cultural Revolution, no human remains were found in it.

ABOVE: Internal view of the Kong Family Mansion.

The Kong Family Mansion lies east of the Confucius Temple and is where the eldest direct male descendant of Confucius lived and worked. First built in the Song Dynasty, it went through continuous renovation and expansion, the present mansion stretches over thirty-three acres. There are 480 rooms with integrated offices and residences. A typical feudal lord's manor, the garden at the back of the mansion is particularly serene and quiet.

Also known as the "sacred cemetery of the sage," the Cemetery of Confucius lies outside the northern city gate of Qufu and has been in continuous use for over 2,500 years. It is surrounded by a brick wall over four miles long and contains over 100,000 graves. Between carved statues and pillars lie the remains of Confucius and various members of his family including his son, Kong Li, and his grandson, Kong Ji.

ABOVE: Front gate of the Kong Family Mansion.

RIGHT: Exterior view of the third hall in the Kong Family Mansion.

FAR RIGHT: Aerial photograph of the Temple and Cemetery of Confucius and the Kong Family Mansion.

LEFT: Located in front of the Dacheng Hall, the Apricot Altar is said to be where Confucius preached.

ABOVE: Kuiwen Pavilion is a library in the middle of the Temple.

FAR LEFT: Cloud and dragon stone columns in Dacheng Hall.

ABOVE: The Everlasting Spring Arch at the Cemetery of Confucius.

LEFT: Rear garden in the Kong Family Mansion.

THE POTALA PALACE

THE POTALA PALACE

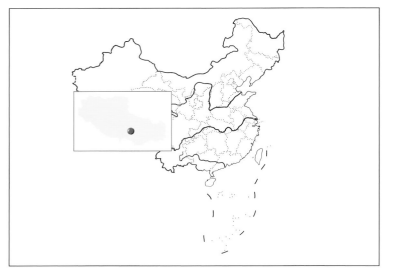

LOCATION: Potala Hill in Lhasa City, Tibet Autonomous Region.

REGISTERED: 1994 (cultural site); expanding to the Zuglakang Monastery in 2000 and to Norbu Lingka in 2001.

The Potala Palace is situated on a hill just over a mile northwest of Lhasa City, capital of the Tibet Autonomous Region. Here, according to Buddhist legend, the Bodhisattva Avalokitesvara lived. He was the bodhisattva who embodies the compassion of all Buddhas. Zigzagging up the hillside, the Potala Palace is built in tiers of red and white painted walls and roofs in dazzling bright colors.

The construction of the Potala Palace began 1,300 years ago in the seventh century A.D. during the reign of the Tibetan king Songtsan Gambo. In the early Tang period, Songtsan Gambo took Princess Wencheng, a daughter of the Tang royal family, as his wife. In order to remember this great event for posterity, he had a nine-story building with a thousand rooms constructed on Red Hill to house the princess. According to historical documents, the hill was walled in three circles, within which the palaces of Songtsan Gambo and that of Princess Wencheng were linked by a silver and copper bridge.

PREVIOUS PAGES: Perched upon Marpo Ri hill, 425ft. above the Lhasa valley, the Potala Palace rises a further 560ft and is the greatest monumental structure in all of Tibet.

LEFT: Zhongdao Ting (Center of Island Pavilion) of the Mid-lake Palace in Norbu Lingka Park (Treasured Garden), a summer retreat for Dalai Lamas in the west of Lhasa City.

ABOVE: The central part of the Potala is called the "red palace" from its crimson color, which distinguishes it from the rest. It contains the principal halls and chapels and shrines of past Dalai Lamas.

The Potala Palace is a wood and stone structure with foundations inserted directly into rock. Its thirteen-story facade rises tier upon tier up to 360ft. high. All the walls are built of granite and were strengthened with molten iron, making the structure as close to earthquake-proof as anything can be in this area. Buddhist pillars, bottles, makaras (capricorns), and gold-winged birds decorate the roof ridges. The wall surfaces beneath the eaves bear gilt brass ornaments in the shape of Buddhist musical instruments and the Eight Treasures. The pillars and beams are covered with gorgeous paintings and carved designs. The interior layout is a lavishly decorated bizarre layout of rooms and passageways with crisscrossing corridors and unexpected halls.

The whole complex consists of the White Palace—the Dalai Lama's living quarters—in the east; the Red Palace—comprising the halls of Buddhas and that of the Dalai Lamas' burial stupas—in the middle; and white dormitories—for the Dalai's trusty lamas—in the west. In front of the Red Palace is a high white wall, the "Buddha Sunning Platform," where a large embroidered portrait of Buddha used to be hung during Buddhist festivals.

ABOVE: Silver statue of a Dharma guardian deity. The Dharma is one of the jewels of buddhism— the teachings or law as expounded by the Buddha.

ABOVE RIGHT: Legends concerning the rocky hill tell of a sacred cave that was the dwelling place of the Bodhisattva Chenresi (Avilokiteshvara).

RIGHT: The mural-covered walls have blistered and cracked over the years and a restoration project is under way.

ANCIENT BUILDING
COMPLEX IN THE
WUDANG MOUNTAINS

ANCIENT BUILDING COMPLEX IN THE WUDANG MOUNTAINS

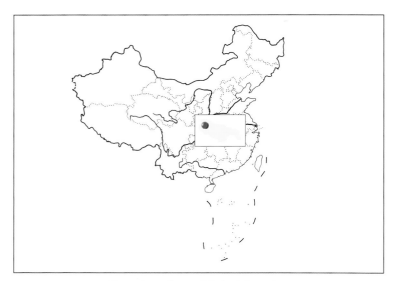

LOCATION: Danjiangkou, Hubei Province.
REGISTERED: 1994 (cultural site).

The Ming emperors called the Wudang Mountains the Mysterious (Xuanyue) or Gigantic (Dayue) Mountains or the Mountains of Supreme Harmony (Taihe). Xu Xiake, the noted Chinese naturalist and geographer (1587–1641), praised them for their beautiful peaks and wonderful landscapes and held them to be above the Five Great Mountains in beauty. This was great praise indeed, for the Five Great Mountains—Taishan, Bei and Nan Hengshan, Huashan, and Songshan—are the sacred mountains of Chinese Taoism.

The first imperial buildings in the area were constructed under the Eastern Han Dynasty (25–220 A.D.); the first religious building, the Five Dragon Temple, under the Tang Dynasty. But it was during the Ming period that the main work took place. Emperor Yongle (1360–1424) ordered the construction of a huge Taoist complex. Overseen by his

PREVIOUS PAGES: Tianzhu Peak, on which the Golden Hall stands, rises 5,290ft. above sea level to provide a perfect vantage point from which to witness magnificent sunrises.

LEFT: One of the best preserved buildings in the Wudang Mountains, Zixiao Palace—at the foot of Zhanqi Peak—was built in 1413, the eleventh year of the reign of Yongle, the third Ming emperor, generally considered one of the greatest of all Chinese emperors.

ABOVE: Xuanyuemen Gate, an exquisitely carved stone archway 67ft. tall and 43ft. wide, is sited at the entrance to Mount Wudang, where the sacred stone stairway to the summit begins.

ministers, hundreds of thousands of soldiers and laborers worked to fulfill his orders. The result was a complex that included palaces, temples, nunneries, and cave-temples. The buildings' locations were chosen with particular attention so that they were in harmony with the natural environment. The buildings are so huge, so perfectly proportioned, and so exquisitely decorated that they have no equal in Taoist China or the rest of the world. Of particular note are the palaces of Taihe (Supreme Harmony), Nanyan (Southern Cliff), Yuzhen (Meeting with Perfect Beings), and Zixiao (Purple Heaven)—the largest complex of buildings. Zixiao Palace is arranged on a five-tier terrace and Zixiao Hall has a wonderful double-caved, hip-and-gable roof.

Other important sites include the remains of the Yuxu (Heaven), Wulong (Five Dragons), and Jindian (Golden Hall) temples. The Golden Hall is a palace-like brass-cast building erected in the Ming period and built to imitate a wooden structure. It is situated in the center of a stone platform built on the summit of Sky-Pillar Peak (Tianzhu), the highest point in the mountains, some 5,290ft. above sea level.

LEFT: Imperial stele in Yuxu Palace. The palace is the most imposing cluster of buildings of the Wudang complex.

RIGHT: The Golden Hall on top of Tianzhu Peak weighs more than 100 tons. There are statues of immortals and animals on the ridges of the double eaves.

BELOW: One of the most magnificent cliff temples of the site is that of Yuxu Cliff, originally built during the Song Dynasty (960–1279 A.D.).

FOLLOWING PAGES: Entrance to the Fuzhen (Truth-Returning) Nunnery. It is said that the god Chenwu stayed at this spot "for self-cultivation." In later years, Mount Wudang was the birthplace of Wudang wushu (martial arts), the most important school of martial arts in south China, practiced by the monks and nuns alike.

FAR LEFT: Nanyan Palace, the most spectacular of the palace locations.

ABOVE: The Dragon-Tiger Hall in Yuzhen Palace. The palace suffered major fire damage in 2003 and is due to be relocated before the Three Gorges Dam is completed in 2010.

LEFT: The Forbidden City in the Wudang Mountains.

215

MOUNT EMEI AND LESHAN GIANT BUDDHA

MOUNT EMEI AND LESHAN GIANT BUDDHA

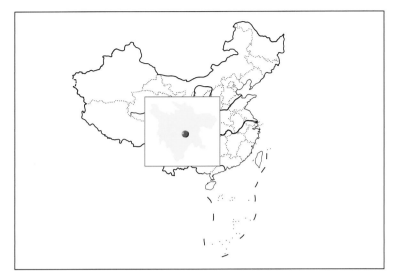

LOCATION: Emeishan City, Sichuan Province.
REGISTERED: 1996 (mixed cultural and natural site).

The Mount Emei Scenic Area covers sixty square miles and is surrounded by a nature reserve over twice as large. This is a wonderful landscape of mysterious beauty, marvelous natural scenery, and an unspoiled environment which—together with its long-standing history and culture—makes it of immense value historically, aesthetically, and scientifically. One of the highlights is the Leshan Giant Buddha, located to the east of Mount Emei, at the confluence of the Minjiang, Dadu, and Qingyi rivers. It took workers ninety years to cut it into the cliffside, and when finished, it measured 233ft.—the tallest stone image of Maitreya (the future Buddha) in the world.

Mount Emei was formed in the late Mesozoic era (around a hundred million years ago) and rises dramatically out of the plain to nearly 8,530ft. It is notable for possessing distinct vertical sequences of soil, climatic, and

PREVIOUS PAGES: The Leshan Giant Buddha, 233ft. tall and the tallest stone Buddha statue in the world.

LEFT: Celestial Mount Emei (the Mountain of Brightness), one of the four sacred Buddhist mountains of China—the others are Wutai in Shanxi, Jiuhua in Anhui, and Putuo in Zhejiang.

ABOVE: The gate of Baoguo Temple. A large engraved stone slab hangs above the gate with the name of the temple written by the Emperor Kangxi (1654–1722).

environmental zones, and so is home to numerous animals and plants. Mount Emei was created by the same massive geological movements that led to the Himalayas and lifted the Qinghai-Tibetan Plateau. The result is a complex geological structure with crisscrossing faults that sees precipitous cliffs, bizarre peaks, and deep valleys. Soil erosion has continued the process, cutting numerous deep gorges.

Mount Emei boasts the most complete subtropical vegetation in the world, as well as an integral vertical sequence of subtropical forest zones formed of (from lower to upper) the evergreen broadleaf forest, evergreen and deciduous broadleaf mixed forest, coniferous and broadleaf mixed forest, and sub-alpine coniferous forest. This constitutes the best-preserved scenery of primitive vegetation in subtropical mountainous areas anywhere in the world.

Ten percent of the total of Chinese plants (some 3,200 species) live on Mount Emei—these include relics of ancient flora such as the dove tree, tetracentraceae, and katsura tree. The Emei flora includes components of both the Sino-Japanese and the Sino-Himalayan floras, and this amalgamation of tropical, subtropical, and temperate floras makes for a peculiar natural landscape.

Mount Emei is home to many species of wild animals, among which are 157 rare local species: twenty-nine are state-protected animals. These include the lesser panda (red panda) and nine species of birds including the honey buzzard and silver pheasant.

Buddhism arrived in China at Mount Emei in the middle of the first century A.D., when Puguang Temple on Golden Summit was built. In the third century, when worship of Buddha Samantabhadra spread into the area, Hui Chi constructed the Samantabhadra Temple (now Wannian Temple) at the foot of Guanxin Hill. In the mid-ninth century, another famous monk, Ji Ye, arrived and built a Buddhist temple where he translated sutras, preached the law, and cast a brass statue of Samantabhadra —62 tons in weight and over 25ft. high.

Thirty temples now remain and many antique treasures have been preserved, including Buddhist scriptures written on pattra, a type of papyrus, a gift presented by the king of Siam during the Ming period.

RIGHT: The Nine-Twist Plank Trail: not a trek for the faint-hearted or those with an aversion to heights.

FAR RIGHT: Another view of the Leshan Giant Buddha. He took ninety years to complete and his smallest toenail is large enough to easily accommodate a seated person.

FOLLOWING PAGES: The grandeur of the Golden Summit. At 10,167ft. above sea level, this is the highest peak on Mount Emei.

ABOVE: China's first Buddhist temple was built on Mount Emei in the first century A.D. Over a hundred temples and halls were built but only twenty now remain.

RIGHT: Bronze statue of Samantabhadra Buddha in Wannian Temple. Standing 24ft. high and weighing 62 tons, this statue was cast in 980 A.D.

224

LEFT: The Leshan Giant Buddha was carved into Lingyun Hill between 713 and 803 A.D. His shoulders are 92ft. wide.

RIGHT: Emei monkeys. The area is home to many plant and animal species, including a number on the verge of extinction.

BELOW: Brick hall in Wannian Temple, the largest temple on Mount Emei, built during the reign of Emperor Long'an of the Eastern Jin Dynasty (397–401 A.D.).

LUSHAN NATIONAL PARK

LUSHAN NATIONAL PARK

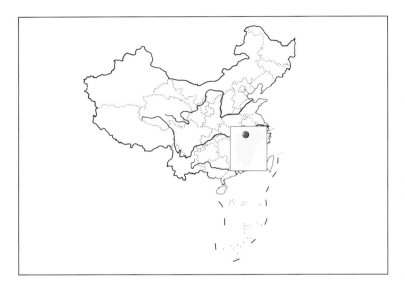

LOCATION: Northern Jiangxi Province.
REGISTERED: 1996 (cultural landscape).

Lushan National Park lies on the southern bank in the middle reaches of China's longest river, the Yangtze, near Poyang Lake, the largest freshwater lake in the country. Mount Lushan is famous for lofty, misty peaks—on average it is clear of clouds for less than half the year.

The north of the park is characterized by the winding Yangtze which forms a series of valleys and mountain ranges, while in the south run fault escarpments, which produce high peaks. Dahanyang Peak, at 4,836ft. above sea level, is the highest point, followed by Tiechuanfeng (Iron Ship Peak) at 3,143ft. Also of note are the Wangjiapo Twin Waterfalls—they look as if the water gushes from the mouths of two dragons—while the Three-Step Waterfall rushes down into a pool from a height of 509ft.

The cool and cloudy Lushan summers are ideal for temperate plants making the Lushan Botanical Garden an

PREVIOUS PAGES: Lake Poyang is is fed by the Gan and Xiu rivers, which connect to the Yangtze.

LEFT: With waterfalls, lakes, and ponds, Lushan National Park boasts some of the most spectacular scenery in China. These lakeside villas provide a tranquil setting to enjoy the view.

ABOVE: Clouds over Hanpo Gorge. Hanpo valley is the best place to watch sunrise and the sea of clouds.

important base for the protection of plant species in the middle and lower reaches of the Yangtze River. The area is of particular importance for birds—over one million migratory birds spend the winter under state protection at Poyang Lake; at least ninety-five percent of the worldwide population of white cranes can be found here.

As described by World Heritage Committee, "Mount Lushan, in Jiangxi, is one of the spiritual centers of Chinese civilization. Buddhist and Taoist temples, along with landmarks of Confucianism, where the most eminent masters taught, blend effortlessly into a strikingly beautiful landscape which has inspired countless artists who developed the aesthetic approach to nature found in Chinese culture."

The White Deer Cave College, first set up in 940 A.D., tops the list of the four largest colleges in ancient China. It was here that Zhu Xi (1130–1200), the master of the neo-Confucian school of the Song Dynasty, advocated his ideas on education. These became the norm in ancient Chinese education and had an important impact throughout the world.

In 391 A.D. the eminent Buddhist leader Huiyuan (334 –416 A.D.) built the Donglinsi (East Grove Temple) at Mount Lushan, and in doing so created a famous temple garden. Huiyuan spent many years of his active life devoted to Buddhism in Lushan, founding the Pure Land Sect— a devotional branch of Buddhism focused on Amitabha Buddha. It is characterized by the assurance of rebirth into the Pure Land the moment one first has faith in Amitabha.

In the wake of the Ming and Qing dynasties Muslims, Protestants, and Catholics also built mosques or churches in Lushan. Over its 1,600 years of development, Lushan has become a rare place where five religions exist side by side on one mountain.

ABOVE: Buddhist monks at the East Grove Temple, at the foot of Xianglu Peak.

RIGHT: The Three-Cascade Waterfall originates on Dayue Mountain, angles around the back of Five-Old-Men Peak, and pours into Nine-Tier Gully.

ABOVE: The Wangjiapo Twin Waterfalls are one of
Lushan's great natural attractions.

ABOVE: Sunset over Mount Lushan and Lake Poyang.

PAGE 236–237: Mount Lushan has inspired many celebrated poets and writers who have been entranced by the mountain's beauty. There are over 400 inscriptions on the cliffs an rocks of the "Mountain of Poetry."

ABOVE: The granite Goddess of Mercy Bridge, almost 82ft. long, is over a thousand years old, and was constructed without using mortar.

RIGHT: Scissors Pass lies north of Guling Town, a unique city set at an altitude of 3,829ft. surrounded on three sides by mountains.

THE OLD CITY OF LIJIANG

THE OLD CITY OF LIJIANG

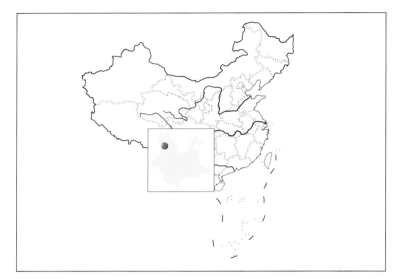

LOCATION: Lijiang Naxi Autonomous County, Yunnan Province.
REGISTERED: 1997 (cultural site).

The Old City of Lijiang is situated in Yunnan Province, on a plateau overlooked by Jade Dragon (Yulong) Mountain. It was first settled in the late twelfth to mid-thirteenth century (at the end of the Song/beginning of the Yuan period), and is often called the "Venice of the East" because of the charms of its water courses. "The palaces are so magnificent as to be comparable with a king's!" exclaimed Xu Xiake, the great Ming traveler, in admiration.

The old city covers one and a half square miles. In the north is the market quarter with Rectangular (Sifang) Street at the center, from which four streets fan out in different directions, each flanked by shopfronts. The eastern city was the location of the liuguan's yamen (office of the non-native governor appointed by the imperial court), where the Civilization (Wenming) Archway, Wenmiao Temple (for the worship of Confucius), and

Wumiao Temple (for the worship of General Guan Yu of the Three Kingdoms Period) still stand.

Ethnically, Lijiang is populated by the Naxi—an ethnic group that lives in the foothills of the Himalayas in Yunnan and Sichuan provinces. But over the years it has combined the essence of the Han, Bai, Yi, and Tibetan peoples—and as the UNESCO description says—it is noteworthy for, "blending of elements from several cultures that have come together over many centuries."

The people of Lijiang built their homes in a unique style, which developed in the light of the specific conditions and traditional customs. This, along with the traditions of ancient architecture in the Central Plains and construction styles of the Bai and Tibetan ethnic groups, meant dwellings included sunshades, storm-resistant roofs, free ventilation, and unique decoration. The most striking of these characteristics is the plain, natural creativeness displayed in the buildings' adaptability to the terrain. Lijiang has contributed important heritage information for research into the history of Chinese architecture and culture.

Unlike any other royal capital in ancient China, Lijiang was constructed entirely beyond the influence of the imperial building standards. It has neither a neat road network nor awe-inspiring city walls. The whole city is laid out within the natural limitations formed by three mountains and a major river, from which three streams extend through the city and spread into a wide system carrying running water to every house. Streets and alleys form a vein-like network and buildings are erected according to the terrain of the hills and the route of the water courses.

PREVIOUS PAGES: A scene in Lijiang—called the "Venice of the East" due to its system of waterways and bridges.

BELOW: A bird's-eye view of Lijiang which has a history going back more than 800 years and was once a center for trade. Sightseers have to walk the cobbled streets as cars are not allowed in the Old City.

ABOVE: One-third of the town was unfortunately destroyed by an earthquake in February 1996.

ABOVE RIGHT: Waterside houses in Lijiang. The water flows into the city through three channels.

BELOW RIGHT: A family house below Yulong Mountain, the southernmost glacier in the northern hemisphere.

LEFT: Interior view of the Buddhist Wenfeng Temple. Built in 1733, the temple was badly damaged during the Cultural Revolution.

Buildings in old Lijiang.

LEFT: A water scene in Lijiang. There is a sluice-gate on the West River, which allows water to pour into the city for street-washing.

TOP: The snow-covered Jade Dragon Snow Mountain as seen from the Jade Spring Park. The highest peak is Shanzidou at 18,373ft.

ABOVE: The main gate of Wenfeng Temple. In the 1980s, the Chinese government organized the temple's restoration.

PREVIOUS PAGES: Another view of Lijiang's rooftops.

RIGHT: Rectangular Street in the old city of Lijiang, situated on a plateau at an elevation of 8,530ft.

FAR RIGHT: The city is unique as it incorporates both the traditions and architectural styles of north and south China.

BELOW: Five Phoenix (Wufeng) Tower—also called Fayun Pavilion—was built in 1601 and was originally situated in Fuguo Temple. It was moved to Jade Spring Park in 1979 for the convenience of tourists.

THE OLD CITY OF PINGYAO

THE OLD CITY OF PINGYAO

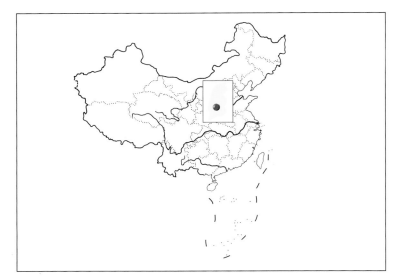

LOCATION: Pingyao County, Shanxi Province.
REGISTERED: 1997 (cultural site).

The Old City of Pingyao in Shanxi Province is a well-preserved historic site and a typical example of an ancient Chinese city. It occupies a total area of a little under a square mile, has a population of 42,000, and—as documentary records and material evidence show—has largely maintained its historical appearance since rebuilding took place during the Ming Dynasty (c.1370 A.D.). The substantial cultural remains preserved in the old city not only represent architectural styles, construction methods, and materials, but also mirror artistic advances and aesthetic achievements of ancient China's ethnic groups in different regions.

Built in King Xuan's reign (827–782 B.C. of the Western Zhou Dynasty), Pingyao has a history of more than 2,700 years and shows the traditional planning principles and building styles of the Han people, particularly the historical features Han culture between the fourteenth and

PREVIOUS PAGES: Pingyao was the financial center of China in the late Qing Dynasty, when there were as many as twenty financial institutions within the city, comprising more than half of total in the whole country.

LEFT: The city wall of Pingyao at sunset. The wall is the most important of Pingyao's treasures.

ABOVE: There are seventy-two watchtowers on the top of the city walls—representing seventy-two people of great wisdom—and 3,000 crenellations (battlements) representing the 3,000 disciples of Confucius.

nineteenth centuries. It is of considerable importance in the research into social, economic, military, religious, ideological, and moral concepts of the time.

Since the establishment of the prefecture and county system in ancient China in 221 B.C., Pingyao has continuously been a county seat, a city at the lowest basic level. The city walls date from the third year of the Hongwu reign during the Ming Dynasty (1370 A.D.). The walls measure about 40ft. high, with a perimeter of 3.75 miles. A 13ft. wide, 13ft. deep moat can be found just outside the walls. In 2004, part of the southern wall collapsed. It has been reconstructed but the rest of the city walls are still largely intact and are considered among the most well-preserved ancient city walls of this scale.

Within the walls remain six temple complexes, county administrative offices, and a city tower—all original structures from different periods. Over a hundred well-preserved streets and alleys are flanked by commercial shops mostly built during the period between the seventeenth and nineteenth centuries; this includes 3,797 traditional-style shops among which over 400 are particularly valued for their unique local features.

The major residences of the Pingyao people were built between 1840 and 1911. Many are adorned with exquisite wooden, brick, and stone carvings and lifelike paper-cut window designs with a strong local flavor.

LEFT: Clay statues in Ten-Thousand-Buddha Hall at Pingyao's Zhenguo Temple—first built in 963 A.D.

ABOVE: Colored statue of Isvara Avalokitesvara— "Lord of all that is seen"—at Pingyao's Shuanglin (Double Tree) Temple.

LEFT: The City Tower, an impressive three-story wooden structure, straddles the main thoroughfare. ABOVE: The city wall is wide on top; and made of compacted earth covered by bricks and stones.

LEFT: Colored statue of Weito (the guardian facing the main hall) in Shuanglin Temple. The temple houses 2,000 Ming and Yuan statues.

TOP: An interior view of the courtyard in a typical family house in Pingyao, nicknamed "tortoise city," symbolizing its longevity and solidity.

ABOVE: Glazed-tile roof of the Temple of the City God that was built during the Northern Song Dynasty (960–1127).

CLASSICAL GARDENS
IN SUZHOU

CLASSICAL GARDENS IN SUZHOU

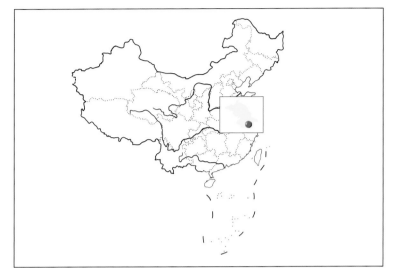

LOCATION: Suzhou City, Jiangsu Province.

REGISTERED: 1997 (cultural site); expanding to the Canglangting Garden (Surging Wave Pavilion Garden), Shizilin Garden (Lion Forest Garden), Yipu Garden (Art Orchard), Ouyuan Garden (Twin Garden), and Tuisiyuan Garden (Garden of Retreat and Contemplation) in 2000.

Suzhou is a city with a long history on the lower reaches of the Yangtze River and on the shores of Lake Taihu. Strategically located on a major trade route—the Grand Canal from Beijing to Hangzhou—Suzhou has also been an important center for China's silk industry since the Song Dynasty (960–1279), and continues to hold that prominent position today.

But it is for its gardens that Suzhou became a World Heritage Site and is often called paradise on earth. The origin of the gardens can be traced back to the sixth century B.C., when the King of Wu of the Spring and Autumn Period built his royal garden here. The first recorded private garden is the Pijiangyuan (Territory-Expander's Garden) of Eastern Jin times (fourth century A.D.). Gardening then thrived in successive periods and the famous gardens increased in size and number. During the Ming and Qing periods, Suzhou became one of the busiest areas in China, with private gardens spreading across the city and suburbs.

During the golden period of garden building—primarily between the sixteenth and eighteenth centuries—there were more than two hundred gardens, of which dozens are still well preserved. Each is admirable for its

PREVIOUS PAGES: The Waterside Pavilion in the Lingering Garden, originally built during the reign of Emperor Jia Jing (1522–66) as a private garden for Xu Shitai, a high-ranking official in charge of the emperor's horses and vehicles.

LEFT: North of the pool in the Retired Fisherman's Garden. Many of the gardens here adhere to the concepts of feng shui, yin and yang, and the Taoist principle of merging humanity into nature.

ABOVE: The Little-Flying-Rainbow Bridge in the Humble Administrator's Garden. With a total area of around twelve acres, this is the largest private garden in Suzhou.

imaginative design, inspiring atmosphere, exquisite workmanship, superb artistry, and rich cultural content. Between them these gardens became the ideal model for the numerous classical gardens of Suzhou.

Two distinct categories of Chinese gardens—imperial and private—evolved in Beijing and Suzhou respectively. Because of their diversity in political, economic, cultural,

climatic, and geographic circumstances, the two categories are distinctly different from each other in scale, layout, dimension, style, and color.

Where the imperial gardens are exceptional for their grandeur, neatness, and sumptuous deep colors, conversely Suzhou gardens impress with their small but elegant appearance, light and graceful colors, and boldly expressive style. The Suzhou gardens were built with particular attention to the delicate balance of harmony, culture, and art, and the imperial gardens would be greatly influenced in later years by the bold Suzhou style.

The Suzhou classical gardens are important historical and cultural living documents and give invaluable information about Chinese traditional ideology and culture. Within the limited spaces around the city, builders applied ingenious ideas on a small scale, making less become more. They combined halls, towers, pavilions, and terraces with springs, rockeries, trees, and flowers in imitation of natural landscapes, creating an ideal world with "urban mounts and forests" and natural beauty amid the bustle of city life.

LEFT: The Green-Floating Pavilion in the Humble Administrator's Garden.

TOP: Moon Gate and Stone Bridge in Yipu (Art) Garden. The Moon Gate is the entrance to Qinlu Courtyard.

ABOVE: The Moon- and Breeze-Enjoying Pavilion and Tassel-Washing Waterside Pavilion west of the pool in the Retired Fisherman's Garden.

271

ABOVE LEFT: The courtyard containing the 21ft. tall limestone Cloud-Capped Peak in the Lingering Garden.

BELOW LEFT: Winding Roofed Walkway and Courtyard in the Garden of Retreat and Contemplation.

ABOVE: Steps on the rockery in the Humble Administrator's Garden.

273

PREVIOUS PAGES: Another view of the Humble Administrator's Garden.

FAR LEFT: Pavement in the Lingering Garden. This garden was reduced to ruins during the World War II, but the government restored it to its former splendor in 1953.

LEFT: Waterside pavilion and walkway in the Art Garden. Many of the original features of the garden have been preserved.

BELOW: A corner of Huanxiu Shanzhuang (the Mountain Villa with Embracing Beauty). The limestone mountain was designed by the great Qing master Gu Yuliang (1764–1830).

LEFT: The Hall for the Venerable Elderly in the
Lingering Garden, one of the forty-two rooms and
halls in the garden.

ABOVE: The 23ft. high rockery in the Mountain
Villa with Embracing Beauty is preeminent among
all the man-made mountains in Chinese gardens.

LEFT: The Green-Encompassing Mountain House in the Lingering Garden.

TOP: Courtyard of the Cloud-Ascending Pavilion in the Retired Fisherman's Garden, the smallest of the Suzhou residential gardens.

ABOVE AND RIGHT: Northern Peak (above) and a corner of a courtyard in the Lingering Garden.

FOLLOWING PAGES: Veranda outside a Slanting Bamboo Twig in the Retired Fisherman's Garden, the best preserved of all the classical gardens.

LEFT: A stone bridge over a limestone gully creates a mountainous landscape in the Mountain Villa with Embracing Beauty.

TOP: Waterside Double Corridor in Canglangting Garden (Surging Wave Pavilion Garden), the oldest of the preserved Suzhou gardens.

ABOVE: The winding roofed walkway leads to quiet areas in the northern section of the Lingering Garden.

287

THE *SUMMER* PALACE

THE SUMMER PALACE

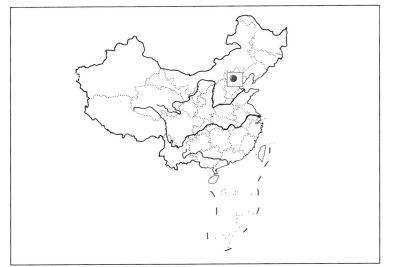

LOCATION: Haidian district, Beijing.
REGISTERED: 1998 (cultural site).

The Summer Palace was built during a flourishing period of the Qing dynasty (1644–1911). Originally called Qingyiyuan Garden (Garden of Clear Ripples), its formal name was changed to Yiheyuan Garden in 1888. Work started on the garden in 1750, the fifteenth year of the reign of Emperor Qianlong and construction of this quintessential celebration of Chinese garden techniques took fifteen years.

It was time well spent! The Summer Palace is one of the best-preserved imperial gardens in China today. Its size is immense and it has an unparalleled beauty as well as a huge collection of precious relics. It marries China's feudal concepts of social status, philosophy, religious belief, and the belief in the contrast of *yin* and *yang* or the substantial and insubstantial all are harmoniously embodied in the buildings and garden.

Unfortunately, both of the most magnificent imperial gardens in China—the Qingyiyuan Garden and the Yuanmingyuan Garden (Garden of Perfection and Brightness) northwest of Beijing—were destroyed by Anglo-French forces in 1860. Some years later (1886) the Qing government had the Qingyiyuan Garden rebuilt with funds originally meant for building China's navy. When it was completed two years later, it acquired its present name, Yiheyuan Garden, and became a retreat for the Empress Dowager Cixi to enjoy in her later years. Ruined in 1900, it was rebuilt again in 1902. The garden became the venue for the political activities of the Qing government toward the end of the dynasty; the Empress Dowager Cixi and Emperor Guangxu attended court affairs there, issued orders, and received foreign envoys.

The Summer Palace covers an area of 716 acres, three quarters of which is surrounded by water. It consists of two major sections: to the north is Wanshou Hill (Hill of Longevity) and in the south lies Kunming Lake which forms a natural boundary on the eastern, western, and southern sides of the garden. The buildings in the Summer Palace can be divided into three groups: the palace quarter, the residential quarter, and buildings in scenic areas.

Along the northern bank of the lake lies the Long Corridor, a 2,388ft. long roofed walkway decorated with colorful paintings that links all the important building groups along the lakeside. The north–south central axis on the southern slope begins with the archway Yunhui Yuyu (Splendid Clouds and Jade Roofs) on the side of the lake. To its north are the Paiyun Men (Cloud-Dispelling Gate), Second Palace Gate, Paiyun Dian (Cloud-Dispelling Hall), Dehui Dian (Hall of Virtue and Light), Foxiangge (Tower of the Fragrance of Buddha), and Zhihuihai (Hall of the Sea of Wisdom) on top of the hill.

PREVIOUS PAGES: A view of the Summer Palace with Kunming Lake, Longevity Hill, and more than 3,000 ancient buildings.

BELOW: The Seventeen-Arch Bridge is 492ft. in length—the largest and longest stone bridge in the Summer Palace—and connects the eastern shore of Kunming Lake and Nanhu Island.

ABOVE: Cloud-Dispelling Hall and Kunming Lake viewed from the Tower of the Fragrance of Buddha on the front slope of Longevity Hill.

RIGHT: The Long Gallery is 2,388ft. in length, has 213 bays, and is decorated with over 10,000 color paintings.

ABOVE: The Hall of Benevolence and Longevity—
where Emperor Guangxu and the Empress
Dowager attended to court affairs and business.

LEFT: Baoyunge Bronze Pavilion of Precious
Clouds, 24ft. high and cast in its entirety from
207 tons of bronze.

ABOVE: Virtuous Wind Hall. The Empress
Dowager Cixi embezzled navy funds to reconstruct
the palace and gardens for her own benefit.

ABOVE: Castle of Cloud-Entertaining Eaves—another of the distinctive buildings that make up the Summer Palace complex.

RIGHT: The Marble Boat, a two-storied boat-shaped building also known as "Qingyanfang" (Boat of Clearness and Comfort).

LEFT: The Garden of Harmonious Interests (Seasons, Water, Bridge, Calligraphy, Pavilion, Corridor, Painting, and Imitation), an exquisite "garden within the garden." A favorite fishing haunt of the Empress Dowager Cixi, it is alleged that eunuchs secretly dived into the water and hung live fish on her hook to keep her in a good mood.

BELOW: Interior view of the Hall of Benevolence and Longevity. Built in 1750, as with much of the palace, it was burned down in 1860 by Anglo-French forces, and later reconstructed.

BELOW LEFT: Revolving Archive, a Buddhist hall. The characters inscribed on the stone tablet are in the handwriting of Emperor Qianlong recording the building of the lake and hill.

FAR LEFT: Back Lake—behind Longevity Hill and formed by the water of Kunming Lake—in the light of the rising sun.

ABOVE: Jade Belt Bridge at the southern tip of the gardens—one of the six bridges on the West Causeway.

LEFT: Bird's-eye view of the building complex that consists of Cloud-Dispelling Hall and Tower of the Fragrance of Buddha.

THE TEMPLE OF HEAVEN

THE TEMPLE OF HEAVEN

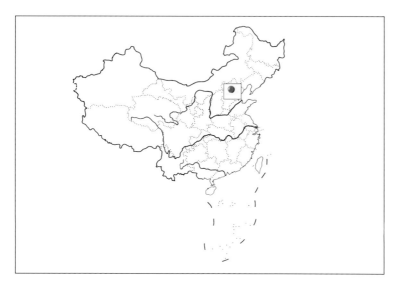

LOCATION: Chongwen district, Beijing.
REGISTERED: 1998 (cultural site).

Situated in the Chongwen district of Beijing, the Temple of Heaven was where emperors paid homage to Heaven and prayed for good harvests in the Ming (1368–1644) and Qing (1644–1911) dynasties. First built in the eighteenth year of the Yongle reign of the Ming dynasty, the Temple of Heaven is China's best-preserved ancient religious building complex.

The site, planning, and architectural design of the temple, the ritual ceremonies and music employed for the worship were all in accordance with the ancient Chinese philosophical theory of Yin and Yang and the theory of the "Five Elements" advocated in the *Book Of Changes*. This was the ultimate expression of man's understanding of Heaven in ancient times, his belief in the oneness of "Heaven and man," and his prayer for the blessing of Heaven.

PREVIOUS PAGES: The Hall of Prayer for Good Harvests has three layers of eaves. Originally, the eaves were painted in different colors. The top was blue, which symbolized Heaven; the middle was yellow to symbolize the emperor; and the bottom was green to represent commoners.

LEFT: A bird's-eye-view of the Temple of Heaven, built in 1420 during the Ming Dynasty to offer sacrifice to Heaven. The design reflected an ancient Chinese thought that "heaven is round and the earth is square."

ABOVE: Gate of the Hall of Abstinence, located near the western entrance of the temple. Emperors of the Ming and Qing dynasties held a three-day fast during summer and winter solstice, the first two days of which were completed at the Forbidden City.

In ancient China, the ritual and ceremonial buildings for the specific use of emperors to worship Heaven and Earth and other deities were referred to as Ming Tang (luminous building). The artistic and architectural technique of the Ming and Qing dynasties reached its peak with the design and construction of the Temple of Heaven. The Hall of Prayer for Good Harvests and the Imperial Heavenly Vault are both colossal wooden circular structures. The vast expanse of trees in the temple grounds were planted to create an environment where nature and man exist in harmony. It is the most outstanding example of imperial, ritual, and ceremonial buildings, and a prime subject for the study of ancient Chinese architecture.

The use of symbolic shapes, numbers, and colors were typically incorporated into ancient Chinese buildings: the number nine was used repeatedly in the number of elements in the Circular Terrace to symbolize Heaven and the link between Heaven and man. The number of columns in the hall symbolizes the four seasons, the twelve months in a year, the twenty-four seasonal division points, and the twelve two-hour periods in a day (as the day was divided in ancient times). The entire building is elaborate with intrinsic meanings to symbolize Heaven and Earth.

FAR LEFT: The ceiling of Qiniandian, the Hall of Prayer for Good Harvests. The four large pillars are known as the Dragon Well Pillars, each represents one of the four seasons.

LEFT: Two stone pavilions were constructed: the right pavilion kept time while the left one was a reminder to the emperor to observe fasting rules.

BELOW: Well Pavilion outside the Divine Kitchen. The water from the well tastes sweet and was used to make soup for sacrificial rituals.

FOLLOWING PAGES: The Hall of Prayer for Good Harvests, a big palace with a round roof and three layers of eaves.

FAR LEFT: Panoramic view of the Altar of Prayer for Grain at the northern end of the complex.

ABOVE: The Circular Mound Altar at the south of the complex, also known as Heaven Mound Altar. It is sixteen feet high and around each of the three tiers are white marble barriers.

LEFT: Within the courtyard of the Circular Mound Altar is a round hall where the spirit tablet of the heavenly god is placed.

FAR LEFT: The vast expanse of cypress trees in the temple grounds.

ABOVE: Panoramic view of the Hall of Abstinence, a building with a white marble foundation constructed entirely from bricks without any pillars or beams.

LEFT: The bells in the tower would ring when the emperor left the Hall of Abstinence and would continue ringing until the emperor arrived at the Circular Mound Altar.

DAZU STONE CARVINGS

DAZU STONE CARVINGS

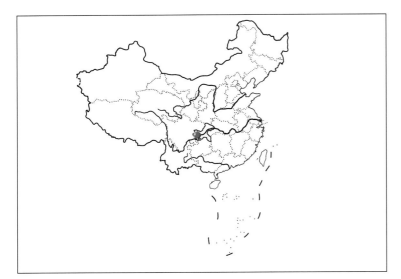

LOCATION: Dazu County of Chongqing Municipality, Sichuan Province.
REGISTERED: 1999 (cultural heritage).

The Dazu stone carvings in Dazu County in Chongqing are some of the finest examples of China's magnificent grotto art. Cut into the mountain cliffs they are important, as the World Heritage Sites description outlines, for their " aesthetic quality, their rich diversity of subject matter . . . and the light that they shed on everyday life in China during this period. They provide outstanding evidence of the harmonious synthesis of Buddhism, Taoism and Confucianism."

The stone carvings first appeared during the Tang Dynasty in Yonghui's reign (650–655 A.D.) and continued through to the final Chinese imperial dynasty, the Qing—although the main period of work was between the ninth and thirteenth centuries. Today this wonderful site has seventy-five area of cliff statues with over 50,000 statues and more than 100,000 inscriptions. The stone carvings on the cliffs of Beishan (North Hill), Baodingshan (Baoding

PREVIOUS PAGES: One of the more than 50,000 stone sculptures: part of the story of the Amitayur Dhyana Sutra about Queen Vaidehi, who finds salvation through Faith. To be found on Beishan (North Hill), it dates from the end of the ninth century.

LEFT: The Buddhist wheel of life on Baodingshan (Baoding Hill), Carved between 1174 and 1252, the wheel is divided into six worlds: devas or gods; asuras (demigods, titans, fighting demons); humans; animals; pretas (hungry ghosts); and hell.

ABOVE: Amputation Hell, one of the gorier images in Dafowan on Baodingshan.

Hill), Nanshan (South Hill), Shizuanshan (Shizuan Hill), and Shimenshan (Stone Gate Hill) are all protected by the state. Grand in scale and rich in content, they are great artistic masterpieces. On the North Hill the statues are built along the cliffs in closely lined shrine caves that makes the area look like a honeycomb.

The statues in Dafowan on Baoding Hill are particularly powerful and magnificent, the best preserved and most densely distributed. The carvings in this huge (100ft. high and over 1,500ft. long) and unique site are by Tantric Sect Buddhists and were cut over a period of seventy years. Their beauty lies not only in the statues, but also their meanings. The stories told by the carvings preach the Buddhist philosophy of life.

Elsewhere, the cliff statues on South Hill, Shizuan Hill, and Stone Gate Hill are all carved with particular care. This group of statues embodies the harmonious integration of Buddhism, Taoism, and Confucianism—something rarely seen in China's cave-temple iconography. Here, uniquely, Buddhist, Confucian, and Taoist statues frequently appear together. In some places they are placed together in positions of equal importance, showing that in this period Confucius, Laotzu, and Sakyamuni were all regarded as equally great sages.

ABOVE: Niche of Thousand-armed Avalokitesvara (who embodies the compassion of all Buddhas); Beishan (North Hill), carved c. 907–965 A.D.

RIGHT: Statue of Manjusri (the bodhisattva of keen awareness); Beishan (North Hill), dated to 1142–1146 A.D.

LEFT: The bodhisattva Avalokitesvara—also known as Guan Yin in East Asia—is generally represented as female. Carving dated around 1142–1146 A.D.

TOP: Niche No.180 on Beishan (North Hill) has been dated to around 1116–1122 A.D.

ABOVE: Disciples attending Sakyamuni (another name for Siddhartha Gautama) entering nirvana; from Baodingshan dated around 1174–1252 A.D.

LEFT: Statue of Jade Seal Avalokitesvara (the Lord who looks down on the world); Beishan (North Hill), 1142–1146 A.D.

ABOVE: Niche of three saints of the Huayan Sect; Dafowan of Baodingshan, 1174–1252 A.D.

ABOVE: Male Attendant to Avalokitesvara; Beishan (North Hill), 1142–1146 A.D.

RIGHT: This carving is named "Nine dragons bathing the prince"; Baodingshan, 1174–1252 A.D.

RIGHT: Colorful and dynamic, this group of statues shows life in heaven, hell, and on earth.

WUYISHAN MOUNTAINS

WUYISHAN MOUNTAINS

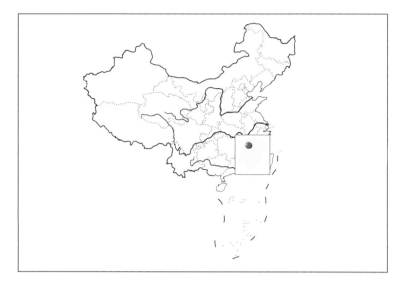

LOCATION: Southern suburb of Wuyishan City, Fujian Province.

REGISTERED: 1999 (mixed cultural and natural site).

The Wuyishan Mountains became a World Heritage Site for many reasons. First, they provide the most important area of biodiversity in southern China. From meadow steppe to temperate coniferous forest, the area is important for its range of trees—in particular the rainforest and also for its evergreen broad-leaved forests, some of which make up the largest remaining tracts of humid subtropical forests in the world.

Second, tea-drinkers around the world recognize the importance of the area: many types of tea are produced around Mount Wuyi, and the slopes of the mountain are where Da Hong Pao and Lapsang souchong tea were first grown. But it is not just the flora that is important: the fauna of the area is prolific with over 5,000 different species recorded—including rare and endangered species such as the South Chinese Tiger (*Panthera tigris amoyensis*), Clouded Leopard (*Neofelis nebulosa*), and Bamboo Snake (*Pseudoxenodon karlschmidti*).

PREVIOUS PAGES: Jade Maiden Peak—fair, slim, and graceful. The nature reserve occupies an area of about 140,850 acres, is on average 3,937ft above sea level, and has the most typical and best-preserved humid sub-tropical native forest in the world.

LEFT: Stone carvings on Wanduifeng Peak (Qing Dynasty, 1644–1911). Wuyi Mountain is known for being of great historic and cultural importance with relics dating back 2,000 years.

ABOVE: Rafting on the Nine-Bends Brook where the water is emerald green and crystal clear. The beauty of the area has given Wuyi the reputation of being the most attractive mountain in southeast China.

Finally, there are also strong cultural reasons for the area to be listed as a World Heritage Site. Preserved in the mountains are ancient sites of the Min and Yue peoples from the second century B.C.—including Hancheng City. But the main cultural interest in the area is its ancient religious heritage: Taoism, Buddhism, and Confucianism have coexisted here in harmony for many years. The mountains have historically attracted Confucian scholars giving doctrinal lectures, starting with King Guye of the Chen period (557–589 A.D.); other Confucian scholars followed such as Yang Shi, Hu An'guo, and Zhu Xi of the Song Dynasty (960–1279). Thanks to them the mountains became the main cultural and academic center in southern China—and since the eleventh century, for Neoconfucianism in particular. Zhu Xi was an unorthodox proponent of this doctrine and would become well regarded after his death.

As early as the Qin (221–207 B.C.) and Han (202 B.C.–A.D. 220) periods, emperors conferred honors on the Wuyishan Mountains. These are recorded in stone carvings—there are over 400 in the area. Emperor Wudi (140–87 B.C.) of the Han Dynasty set up an altar here to offer sacrifices to Wuyi Jun, the God of Wuyishan Mountains. Ever since these mountains have seen significant Taoist and Buddhist centers—there are nearly 300 temples and nunneries in the area.

FAR LEFT: Ruiquan (Auspicious Spring) Waterfall. Most of the hills are formed from red sandstone and are very steep but flat on top.

LEFT: Tourists enjoy the magnificent scenery on board a raft in front of Jade Maiden Peak, Wuyi's most distinctive landmark.

BELOW LEFT AND BELOW: Wuyi Canyon is almost nine miles long and the aptly named Nine-Bend River (Jiuqu Xi) is some forty miles in length.

FAR LEFT: Water Curtain Cave, the largest rock cavern in the mountains where two streams drop from the precipice like strings of pearls.

LEFT: Immortals fishing in the fairyland. The mountains cover an area of twenty-three square miles.

FAR LEFT: Chongyou Taoist Temple (from the Southern Tang Dynasty, 937–975 A.D.) is the only remaining structure—apart from two wells—of the three hundred-room Chongyou Wanniangong (Palace of Ten Thousand Years).

LEFT: Snowflake Spring, one of the more popular atttractions in the Cloud Nest-Tianyou Scenic Area of the Wuyi Mountains.

BELOW: Splendors of Tianyou Peak (Peak of Sky Tour) which is frequently draped in a sea of clouds.

LEFT: Mountains and waterways interlock with each other in a way that typifies the landscape in this region.

TOP: Turtles in and out of water. Shui Jin Gui is a famous Wuyi blend of tea whose name means Golden Marine Turtle.

ABOVE: The Nine-Dragon Nest valley is full of tea trees, including the Red Robe Tea Tree known as the "King of Tea Trees."

LONGMEN GROTTOES

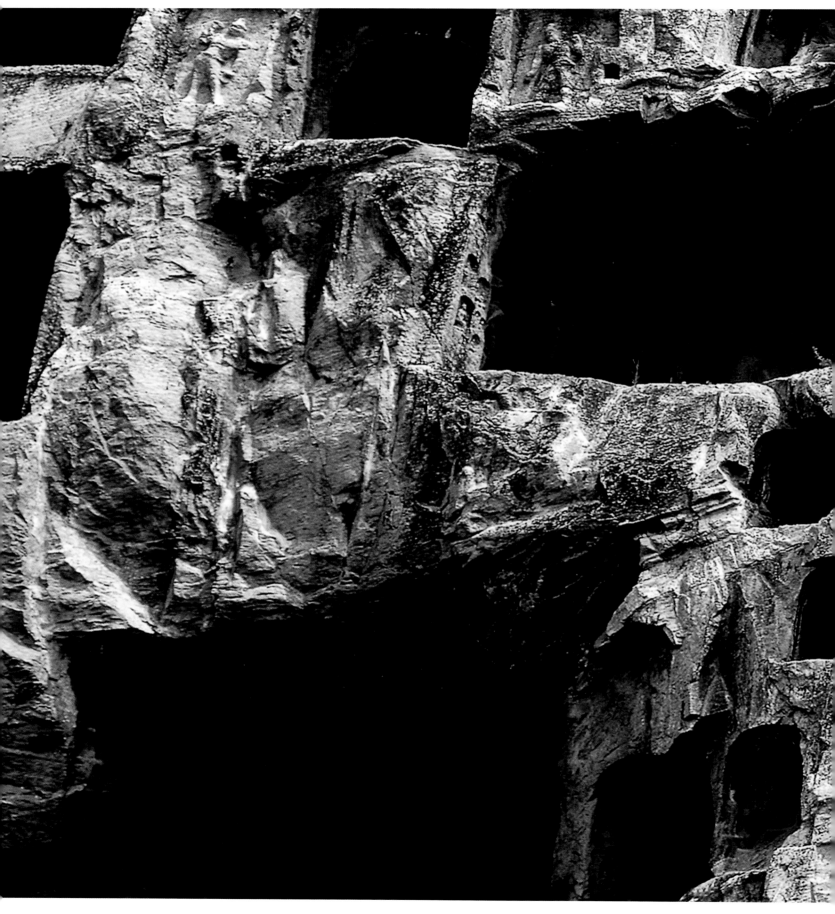

LONGMEN GROTTOES

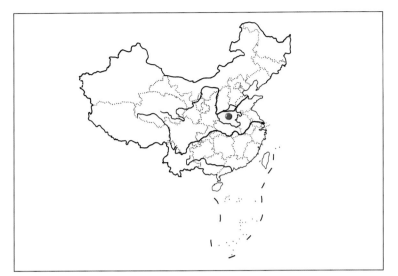

LOCATION: Eight miles to the south of Luoyang City, Henan Province.

REGISTERED: 2000 (cultural site).

The Longmen Grottoes can be found some eight miles south of China's historic city of Luoyang—the eastern capital of the country during the Tang Dynasty. Together with the Mogao Caves in Dunhuang and the Yungang Grottoes in Datong, the Longmen Grottoes are one of the most important homes of Buddhist cave-temple art in ancient China.

The sheer quantity of objects on the site is remarkable: there are 2,345 caves or niches that contain over 100,000 statues and images, and more than 30,000 engraved inscriptions compressed into an area extending north to south for a little over half a mile.

Construction of the grottoes themselves began in 493 A.D. when Emperor Xiaowen of the Northern Wei Dynasty (386–534 A.D.) moved the capital to Luoyang, around the same time that the Shaolin Temple was constructed in the region. Work on the caves continued for some 400 years,

PREVIOUS PAGES: A panoramic view of the Longmen grottoes—a treasure trove of ancient Buddhist art.

OPPOSITE AND ABOVE: The oldest and largest of the Longmen Grottoes is Guyangdong Cave which dates to around 493–534 A.D. It is extremely detailed with row upon row of niches carved into the walls.

the bulk being produced under the Tang Dynasty (618–907). Most of the caves were built with funds from the imperial family and other court notables.

The first cave to be cut was Guyangdong Cave. This has three tiers of niches on its northern and southern walls, in which are hundreds of statues, and most of the statues are engraved with the names of the artists, the dates, and the reasons for carving them. But it is the Binyangzhongdong Cave (Middle Binyang Cave), worked in the sixth century, that tops the rest for decoration. Created between 500 and

523 A.D., there are eleven big statues, the floor is engraved with lotus patterns, and on the rooftop is a relief of a flourishing lotus flower. It is, however, the Giant Statue Niche in Fengxiansi Cave that is the largest in terms in scale. Its main statue, Buddha Rocana, measures over 56ft. The cave was excavated during the Tang Dynasty and it is about 118ft. by 136ft. As well as the Buddha, Fengxiansi has other major figures: there are statues of two of Buddha's disciples, Kasyapa and Ananda, as well as a variety of Bodhisattvas and devas.

Other caves worthy of mention are: Lianhua (Lotus) Cave with a large lotus flower on its ceiling. This cave dates to 527 A.D. Also of note is Wanfo Cave—also known as the Ten Thousand Buddha Cave. Built during the Tang Dynasty, the cave includes over 15,000 miniature statues of Buddha. The cave's primary Buddha sits on a lotus and is kept company by four guards and two bodhisattvas.

RIGHT AND FAR
RIGHT: Guyangdong
Cave's attendant
Bodhisattva (right)
and Weilingzang
Niche (opposite).
The skill of the
craftsmen is evident
from the masterpieces
they carved out of
the natural limestone
cavern.

LEFT: The main Buddha in the middle of the three caverns that make up the Binyang Caves.

ABOVE: Details of a standing Buddha that dates to around 500–523 A.D. on the south wall of Binyangzhongdong Cave

FOLLOWING PAGES: Statues of Buddha, disciples, bodhisattvas, heavenly kings, and warriors in Fengxiansi Cave.

LEFT: The caisson in Binyangzhongdong Cave forms a marvelous lotus-flower canopy looking down on the main statue of Sakyamuni.

ABOVE: Details of Ananda, student of Buddha, in Fengxiansi Cave, dating from the second year of Shangyuan's reign, 675 A.D.

FOLLOWING PAGES: Massive bodhisattvas in the main grotto.

ABOVE: Bodhisattva Samantabhadra to the south of the main statue in Fengxiansi Cave.

RIGHT: Bodhisattva Manjusri to the north of the main statue in Fengxiansi Cave, the largest open air niche of all the caves in China.

MOUNT QINGCHENG – DUJIANGYAN IRRIGATION NETWORK

MOUNT QINGCHENG – DUJIANGYAN IRRIGATION NETWORK

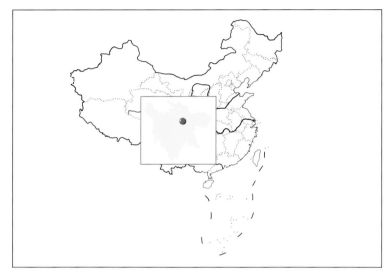

LOCATION: Dujiangyan City, Sichuan Province.
REGISTERED: 2000 (cultural heritage).

Mount Qingcheng has long enjoyed the reputation of being "a retreat with the deepest tranquillity under Heaven," so it is no surprise that this is one of the birthplaces of Taoism, a religion that worships the beauty of nature. It is said that Zhang Ling of the East Han dynasty (25–220 A.D.) started an incense burner on Mount Qingcheng and called the religion "Wudoumi Taoism." From then on, Taoist temples like Jianfu Palace, the Cave of Heavenly Teacher, Palace of Taoist Founder, and Shangqing Temple were built in these mountains. About ten have been well preserved, and together with the beautiful scenery they have attracted countless scholars to write poetry and prose, and to carve inscriptions on the rocks.

The mountain's lower slopes are heavily wooded and the deep green valleys are tranquil and calm—the reason for Qingcheng's soubriquet, "the green city." The main peaks of

rise out of the verdant hillsides tall, elegant, and steep. The main peaks are named for dragons—thus White, Black, Green, Red, and Yellow Dragon Peak provide beautiful views around Mount Qingcheng. There are important Taoist structures on the mountain, such as Jianfu Temple, built in 780 A.D., or the Temple of the Highest Clarity that stands on the eastern hillside of the peak.

Located where the Minjiang River leaves the mountain, the Dujiangyan irrigation network is one of the most remarkable pieces of ancient civil engineering in China and it is easy to understand why it has been listed as a World Heritage Site.

It was built over 2,200 years ago under the direction of Li Bing, governor of Shu Prefecture, in the last year of King ZhaoXiang (256–251 B.C.). Its rationale is quite simple: the high ground of Yulei Mountain stopped the river from reaching Chengdu Plain, and this meant that agricultural development in the region was seriously affected from lack of water. Li Bing, after a careful and thorough survey of the region, had a channel cut through the mountain put a dyke in the middle of the Minjiang River to divide it into two. The channel took water to the plain, which then flourished.

The efficacy of the arrangement is evident: the system is still in use today, channeling water to Chengdu without having to resort to a dam. Few such works of engineering

PREVIOUS PAGES: Two views of Dujiang weir, showing the watershed built in the middle of the Minjiang River to divide it into two parts.

ABOVE: Baopingkou is the entrance of the inner river canal. It is narrow so that the amount of water inflow is controlled.

BELOW LEFT: A snow-covered Mount Qingcheng. The highest point on the mountain is Laoxiaoding Peak at 5,249ft.

LEFT: Bamboo cages loaded with cobbles at Feishayan. These were used in the absence of cement and proved highly effective.

365

RIGHT: The lush green countryside of Mount Qingcheng is a botanical treasure trove that has been studied over the years by those searching for enlightenment, tranquillity—and the secret of immortality.

FAR RIGHT: A stream at the source of the Minjiang River, the longest and largest of the headwaters that feed into the Yangtze River.

BELOW: Instructions and advice for regulating rivers and watercourses are now on display, along with Qing Dynasty maps.

LEFT AND ABOVE LEFT: Qingcheng has the natural habitat of the giant panda, allowing a breeding program to be set up at Wolong Nature Reserve.

TOP: A sea of clouds at Mount Qingcheng, named Green City Mountain because the peaks have been likened to city battlements.

ABOVE: Workshop of Natural Painting. The founder of Taoism, Zhang Daoling, set up his pulpit on the mountain to give lectures.

IMPERIAL MAUSOLEUMS AND MEMORIAL BUILDINGS OF THE MING AND QING DYNASTIES

IMPERIAL MAUSOLEUMS AND MEMORIAL BUILDINGS OF THE MING AND QING DYNASTIES

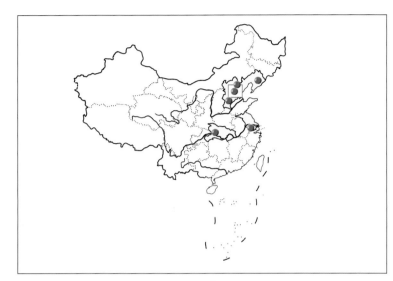

LOCATION: Nanjing City of Jiangsu Province, Beijing City, Zhongxiang City of Hubei Province, Zunhua City and Yixian County of Hebei Province, Shenyang City of Liaoning Province.

REGISTERED: 2002, 2003 (cultural site).

The burial places of the emperors, empresses, and imperial concubines of the two dynasties epitomize the architecture of imperial tombs in feudal China. The rationale for World Heritage Site status is twofold: "harmonious integration of remarkable architectural groups in a natural environment . . . makes the Ming and Qing Imperial Tombs masterpieces of human creative genius" and "outstanding testimony to a cultural and architectural tradition that for over five hundred years dominated this part of the world."

In ancient feudal China, generous burials were thought to show the piety of descendants, and this was especially true in the case of emperors. When an emperor died, a gigantic mausoleum was built for him regardless of cost. It demonstrates the political, moral, and aesthetic ideology of a certain period, and reflects as well the then economic circumstances, scientific and technological level, and architectural achievements.

There is not space to describe in detail all the sites identified in this overall listing. Suffice it to mention as

examples the tombs listed in 2004—three imperial tombs of the Qing Dynasty in Liaoning Province including the Yongling Tomb, the Fuling Tomb, and the Zhaoling Tomb, all built in the seventeenth century. Tied up with this was the Chinese observance the precepts of traditional Chinese geomancy and feng shui theory.

First, Yongling Mausoleum. This is a not large enclosure—the mausoleum, nestled among the hills with Qiyun Mountain towering behind it, is opposite Yancong Mountain with Suzi River running between them. Originally known as Xingjingling, it was built in 1598, and

ancestors of the first Qing emperor, Nurhachi, are buried here.

The Zhaoling Tomb on the other hand is one of the finest sights in Shenyang, the largest and the most complete among the imperial tombs in northeast China. Set in a huge park, the tomb is the burial place of Huangtaiji (1592–1643), eighth son of Nuerhachi, the first Qing emperor, and Empress Boerjiteshi. The tomb took eight years to build (1643–1651) and the impressive animal statues on its approach are reminiscent of Ming tombs.

The overall arrangement of this cemetery is the same as Fuling. The graves are surrounded by rectangular walls, and the red entrance gate is located in south center. The memorial archway lies in the center outside the door. It is exquisitely carved. The left and right walls are inlaid with vividly shaped colored glazed dragons. Inside the door, on the two sides of the Spirit Path, are six pairs of stone sculptures of lions, Chinese unicorns, camels, horses and elephants.

Finally, Fuling Tomb is set in a forested area five miles from Shenyang. Entombed here is Emperor Nuerhachi (1559–1626), the first emperor of the Qing Dynasty, and his Empress Yehenala. Construction started in 1629 and it was expanded during the Kang Xi and Qian Long reigns. Overall, the architecture of the tomb is reminiscent to that of the Forbidden City of Beijing.

ABOVE: Leng'andian hall at Ming Xiaoling Mausoleum, Nanjing, Jiangsu Province. This was built for the first Ming Dynasty emperor, Zhu Yuanzhang.

ABOVE RIGHT: Great Stele Tower in Xiaoling Mausoleum of Ming dynasty, Nanjing, Jiangsu Province.

RIGHT: Three stone memorial archways and the Great Red Gate at Tailing Mausoleum of the Emperor Yongzheng, Yixian county, Hebei Province.

FAR RIGHT: Radiate Tower in Square Bastion in Ming Xianling Mausoleum, Zhongxiang, Hubei Province.

LEFT: Qing Fuling Mausoleum is the tomb of Nurhachi (1559–1626) in Shenyang City, Liaoning Province.

TOP: Leng'endian hall and front square in Qing Fuling Mausoleum, Shenyang City, Liaoning Province.

ABOVE: Main hall of Xiaoling Mausoleum of Emperor Shunzhi, Qing East Mausoleum precinct, Zunhua City, Hebei Province.

OPPOSITE, TOP: Chongling Mausoleum in Qing West Mausoleums precinct, Yixian County, Hebei Province.

FAR LEFT, BELOW: Sacrifice-to-constellation Gate in Ming Xianling Mausoleum, Zhongxiang, Hubei Province.

ABOVE: Tailing Mausoleum—Qing West Mausoleums, Yixian County, Hebei Province—set the tone for the majority of the rest of the tombs in this complex.

LEFT: Bird's-eye view of Qing East Mausoleum precinct, Zunhua City, Hebei Province. This is China's largest and most complete complex of tombs.

ANCIENT VILLAGES IN SOUTHERN ANHUI PROVINCE

ANCIENT VILLAGES IN SOUTHERN ANHUI PROVINCE

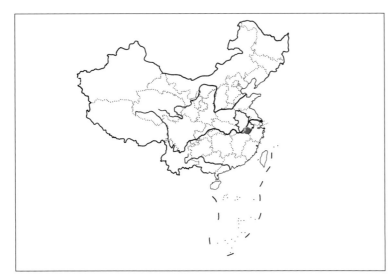

LOCATION: Yixian County, Huangshan City, Anhui Province.
REGISTERED: 2000 (cultural site).

Yixian acquired its status in the Qin dynasty (221 B.C.) more than 2,200 years ago, making it one of the oldest counties in China. There are still as many as 3,500 well-preserved ancient Ming and Qing dynasty dwellings in villages within the county. These dwellings, built by rich Anhui merchants, have strong local characteristics and are permeated with the cultural heritage of Anhui Province. The reasons for their inclusion as World Heritage Sites is that they are "graphic illustrations of a type of human settlement created during a feudal period and based on a prosperous trading economy" and that "traditional non-urban settlements of China, which have to a very large extent disappeared during the past century, are exceptionally well preserved in the villages of Xidi and Hongcun."

The villages were sited based on the theories of feng shui or geomancy according to the *Book of Changes*. According

to this theory, the most ideal site is one that gives full respect to the natural environment so that the "oneness of Heaven and man" can be achieved. Under the guidance of such a theory, the villages were developed to meet both the material and spiritual needs of the residents. The contours of each village is in harmony with its geographical features and natural scenery of mountains and water.

The ancient villages situated to the south of the Yangtze River are characterized by building groups developed before the end of the Qing dynasty. These include vernacular dwellings, family ancestral temples, classical learning schools, memorial arches, pavilions, terraces, and irrigation projects.

First started in 1047 A.D., Xidi village is surrounded on all sides by mountains. Two streams run through it and meet at the Huiyuan bridge. The buildings are wooden with enclosed brick walls and are embellished with wood, stone, and brick carvings. The streets, lanes, streams, and the layout of houses and courtyards are all well-proportioned. The quiet and unsophisticated lanes, the ancient dwellings along the streams, the beautiful private gardens, and the tall memorial arches standing at the entrance of the village give it a unique atmosphere.

Hongcun village was founded in 1131 A.D. Its most distinctive features are its 400-year-old waterways which twist and wind through the village and form two lakes, Moon Lake and South Lake. Running water reaches all houses and the streets and lanes are laid out along the waterways and paved with stone slabs. It is said that the village is arranged in the shape of an ox—the nearby Leigang Hill is the ox's head, its horns being outlined by the two trees standing on it. Four bridges across the Jiyin stream are the animal's legs and the houses of the village form the body. With marbled ground, black tiles, fresh red lanterns, and elaborate wood-carvings the best houses in the village provide the visitor with vernacular architecture's palaces.

PREVIOUS PAGES: The architecture and carvings of many residences in Hongcun village date back to the Ming and Qing dynasties and are said to be among the best of their kind in China.

LEFT: Gigantic ancient tree at entrance of Hongcun village, situated near Mount Huangshan. The layout of the village is said to be based on the form of an ox.

ABOVE: The Virtue Arch devoted to Hu Wenguang, a Qing prefectural governor, stands at the entrance of Xidi village.

ABOVE: You are never far away from water in Hongcun village.

RIGHT AND FAR RIGHT: Decorative stone and wood carvings abound in the vernacular village dwellings.

FOLLOWING PAGES: The architecture of Hongcun and its layout speak of a successful and thriving medieval site.

384

YUNGANG GROTTOES

YUNGANG GROTTOES

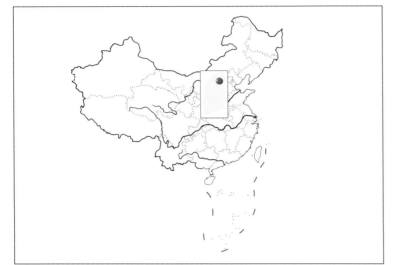

LOCATION: Northern side of the Wuzhoushan Valley, ten miles to the west of Datong City proper, Shanxi Province.

REGISTERED: 2001 (cultural site).

The Yungang Grottoes acquired their name during the Ming Dynasty; originally the complex was called Wuzhoushan Hill Cave Temple. It is one of the earliest examples of Chinese cave-temple art. The grottoes house 252 niches of various sizes and over 51,000 statues. Construction began in the first year of the reign of Heping (460–465 A.D.) during the Northern Wei period. The area enjoyed great prosperity in the last half of the fifth century a period, which lasted till the 520s.

UNESCO's citation points to the fact that the Buddhist tradition of religious cave art achieved its first major impact at Yungang, where it developed its own distinct character and artistic power and that the site represents "the outstanding achievement of Buddhist cave art in China in the fifth and sixth centuries."

The Buddhas are mainly Trikala Buddhas—Buddhas of the past, present, and future. Each has a tall usnisa (crown

PREVIOUS PAGES: Exterior view of the Middle Group of Yungang Grottoes, made up of front and back chambers with Buddha statues in the center. The walls and ceilings are covered with embossing.

LEFT: Exterior view of Grottoes Five, Six and Seven which were created during Phase II (470–494 A.D.), when Emperor Xiao Wen moved the Wei capital from Pingcheng to Louyang.

ABOVE: Main Buddha in the two caves of Grotto 19. The Five Caves created by Tan Yao (Caves Sixteen to Twenty) constitute a classical masterpiece from the first flowering of Chinese Buddhist art.

faced and short-bodied, wearing crowns with fluttering silk ribbons on their heads, jeweled necklaces and strings of ornaments on the body, bracelets on arms and wrists, while the pleats of their garments are moderate in density. The style of these statues reflect traits of the Liangzhou grottoes as well as Gandhara and Gupta iconography.

The Tanyaowuku Grottoes are named after the eminent monk Tan Yao who directed the cutting. With a U-shaped plan and vault, they are rough imitations of ancient Indian thatched cottages, emphasizing an important feature of the grottoes, that this cave art represents the successful fusion of Buddhist religious symbolic art from south and central Asia with Chinese cultural traditions. Each grotto has a door and window and is covered with carvings of Thousand Buddhas all over the outer wall.

of the head) full face, high nose, deep eyes, narrow and long brows and eye-sockets, "A"-shaped mustache, and square shoulders on a strong body. The bodhisattvas are round-

FAR LEFT: The sandstone carvings in the Yungang Grottoes (Cloud Ridge Caves) are most impressive.

LEFT: Stupa-pillar in Grotto 2, carved during the Bei Wei period. In the center is a square tower covered with stories and pictures of the Buddha as are all four of its walls.

BELOW: Grotto 34 in the Western Group. The carving styles and techniques here are more developed than in the eastern and central sections.

ABOVE: Buddha in the upper tier in Grotto 5. The central seated Buddha in this grotto is the tallest statue at Yungang Grottoes at 56ft. high.

RIGHT: Standing Buddha on the Eastern Wall of Grotto 20, which also houses the sitting statute of Sakyamuni.

ABOVE: Exterior view of Grotto 3 demonstrating the scale of the grottoes.

RIGHT: Pavilions in front of Grottoes 5, 6, and entrance gate to the Temple. The carving in these two grottoes are considered to represent the pinnacle of the art at Yungang.

INDEX